Trading with the Enemy

PHILIP LEIGH

# TRADING WITH THE ENEMY

THE COVERT ECONOMY DURING THE AMERICAN CIVIL WAR

WESTHOLME
Yardley

First Westholme Paperback 2022



Westholme Publishing, LLC
904 Edgewood Road
Yardley, Pennsylvania 19067
Visit our Web site at www.westholmepublishing.com

ISBN: 978-1-59416-387-6
Also available as an eBook.

Printed in the United States of America.

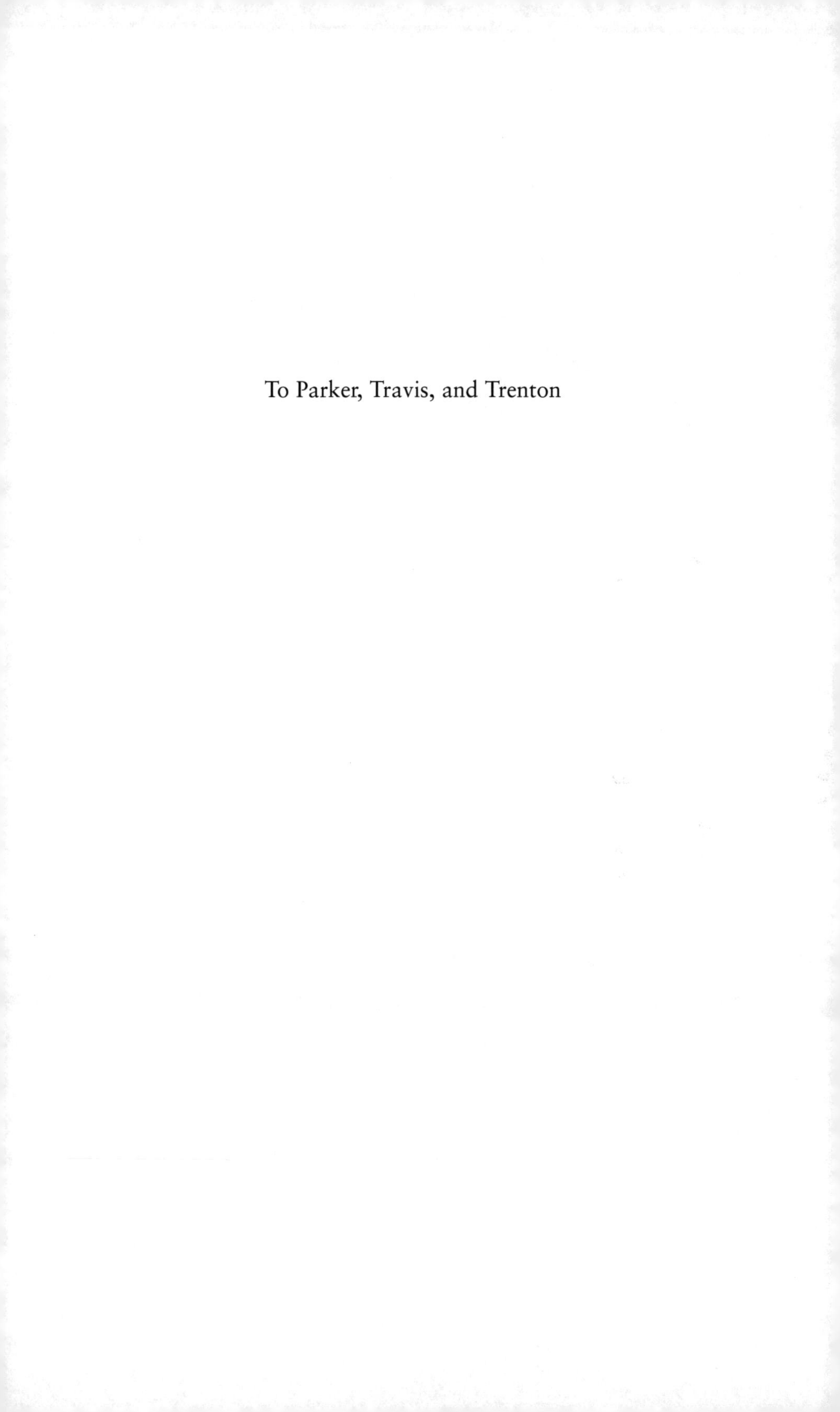

To Parker, Travis, and Trenton

. . . the ways of the dollar were always devious.
—Walter Tevis, *The Hustler*

# CONTENTS

*Maps and Tables*

# INTRODUCTION

On June 7, 1863, the Confederate commerce raider *Clarence* forced the US flagged *Alfred H. Partridge* to stop off the North Carolina coast. The raider anticipated the *Partridge* would be the second of an eventual string of twenty-one prizes. Normally, seized merchant ships were burned or used to transport previously captured crews to a safe harbor. But upon boarding the schooner, the Rebels discovered it was bound for Matamoros, Mexico, out of New York with a cargo of arms and clothing for Texas Confederates. Consequently, the *Partridge* was set free.[1]

Since Matamoros was a neutral Mexican port, federal warships could not blockade it. Before the Civil War, only about one ship annually cleared New York for the Mexican town. However, a year after the war's first important battle at Bull Run, the average was about one per week. Ships to Matamoros were also cleared from Boston, Philadelphia, and other Northern harbors. Cargoes included a multitude of Northern-made items that would have been considered contraband if shipped directly into the Confederacy. They encompassed weapons, munitions, and military uniforms, among other articles. For Northerners willing to help arm the Confederacy for a profit, Matamoros was little more than a legal fig leaf to cover dubious, if not treasonable, conduct.[2]

In exchange, Southern planters provided cotton from fields as far away as Arkansas, Louisiana, and east Texas. They typically loaded wagons with twenty cotton bales and set out in caravans over crude trails ending in Brownsville, Texas, across the shallow Rio Grande from Matamoros. En route teamsters were vulnerable to unpredictable water shortages and attack from hostile Native Americans, and outlaws of all types. Next to gold or specie (gold and silver coins), cotton was the most acceptable international exchange medium available to North Americans, whether in the Union or Confederacy. Adroit, clever, and sometimes ruthless contraband-for-cotton traders accumulated fortunes in Matamoros and Brownsville.[3]

One example was Connecticut-born Charles Stillman, who sold Rebel cotton out of Matamoros to buyers in Northern states, including the US government. His chief cotton supplier was a putative Confederate-loyal Texan who changed sides after federal troops temporarily occupied Brownsville in November 1863. In order to prevent interference from the newly arrived Yankee soldiers, he swore an oath of loyalty to the Union. After the war, Stillman was one of the wealthiest Americans and a major shareholder in New York's National City Bank. His son, a grandson, and a great-grandson each served as National City's board chairman, the great-grandson as late as 1967. Presently, the bank is known as Citicorp. Two of Charles Stillman's granddaughters married into the Rockefeller family.[4]

Despite its legal circumvention advantage, Matamoros was a comparatively minor part of Civil War interbelligerent trade. More often, the exchange was directly across enemy lines. The practice became important about a year after the opening shots at Fort Sumter, in spring 1862, as the cotton-trading centers at New Orleans and Memphis were captured. When Union Major General Benjamin Butler arrived in New Orleans with fifteen thousand occupation soldiers in May 1862, his net worth was about \$150,000, but six years later it was \$3 million. Although the lawyer-general was too shrewd to incriminate himself, there is little doubt the gain was primarily achieved by trade with the enemy.[5] By summer 1862, Union Major General William T. Sherman at Memphis complained that Northern traders were buying Southern cotton for gold, which he believed the Rebels next used to buy weapons at Nassau in the Bahamas and even in Cincinnati. In an August 1862 letter to his brother Senator John Sherman of Ohio, General Sherman wrote, "Cincinnati furnishes more contraband goods than [leading blockade-running port] Charleston, and has done more to prolong the war than the state of South Carolina."[6] A few months later, Major General Ulysses Grant captured Confederate cavalry in northern Mississippi armed with modern carbines evidently purchased at occupied Memphis.[7]

Ladies were not excluded from such trade and were sometimes especially effective. They were generally held less accountable for violations, and soldiers were hesitant to physically search them. For example, while Union Captain Julius Ochs was assigned to a unit guarding the St. Louis-to-Cincinnati railroad, his wife was caught trying to smuggle quinine in a baby carriage across an Ohio River bridge to Rebels in Kentucky. Somehow Captain Ochs got the charges dropped, but his wife's dedication to the South persisted. After the war, she joined the United Daughters of the Confederacy while her husband became a member of the Grand Army of the Republic, a Union veterans organization. Their eldest son, Adolph, became a Chattanooga, Tennessee, newspaperman. Shortly before the turn of the nineteenth to the twentieth century, Adolph bought a failing New York newspaper, added the words "All the News That's Fit to Print" to its masthead, and launched the *New York Times* toward national prominence.[8]

Men are seldom motivated to enlist as soldiers merely to fight a war for economic gain. A higher calling is required to justify leaving their homes and risking their lives in a fight requiring them to shoot to kill strangers who normally have done them no harm. In spring 1861, the concept of "Union" became sufficiently noble to qualify as such a calling in the North. Southerners simply rallied to the equally high-sounding notion of "independence." Both terms were facades. The North wanted an intact Union in order to sustain its emerging economic supremacy, whereas the South wanted independence with slavery.

Without the South's raw materials and favorable export trade balance, business leaders in the North justifiably worried that the economies of the states remaining in the Union after Southern secession might collapse. Ten days before South Carolina led the Southern states into secession on December 20, 1860, the *Chicago Daily Times* editorialized on the calamities of disunion:

> In one single blow our foreign commerce must be reduced to less than one-half what it now is. Our coastwise trade would pass into other hands. One-half of our shipping would be idle. . . . We should lose our trade with the South, with all its immense profits. Our manufactories would be in utter ruins. . . . If [our protective tariff] be wholly withdrawn from our labor . . . it could not compete with the labor of Europe. We should be driven from the market and millions of our people would be compelled to go out of employment.[9]

Such worries had validity, as President Abraham Lincoln hinted in his first inaugural address: "Physically speaking we cannot separate. We cannot remove our respective sections. . . . [The two sides] cannot but remain face-to-face and intercourse, either amicable or hostile, must remain between them."[10] It's unlikely that Lincoln realized just how prophetic his conclusion would become as trade continued—and sometimes even flourished—during four years of bitter warfare between the two regions.

To understand how a dissected Union bereft of between-the-lines trading could lead to economic collapse in the North, it is necessary to examine world cotton markets on the eve of the Civil War, as well as the commercial relations between North and South. Such is the objective of chapter 1. Cotton textile manufacturing was the world's biggest industry, and it was largely dependent upon the Southern states for feedstock. Southern cotton alone accounted for about two-thirds of all US exports.[11] A truncated country composed solely of Northern states could not hope to maintain a favorable international balance of payments. The situation would be exacerbated if the Southern states ceased to be a market for Northern manufactured goods, which would be likely given the Confederacy's adoption of lower import tariffs.[12]

However, the cotton-trading pattern also created intersectional dependencies in the South. The Southern focus on cash crops, such as cotton and tobacco, left it with a need to buy wheat, corn, and pork, which were abundantly available from states northwest of the Ohio River.[13] (Now generally referred to as the Midwest, this area was then known as the Northwest.) Similarly, the South depended on outside sources for nearly all manufactured articles. While such goods could be imported from Europe, protective tariffs in the United States often made domestically produced alternatives from the North more economical. Initially, the South required provender from the Northwest more than the North needed cotton. That changed quickly as New England's cotton inventories dwindled and Lincoln discovered he could use the purchase of the staple to curtail the outflow of gold from the Treasury because cotton could be exported for exchange credits abroad.

Because trade between the belligerents was almost a certainty, chapter 2 describes the regulations each side adopted in efforts to control it in a manner optimal to its interests. Generally, Confederate president Jefferson Davis looked the other way out of necessity, whereas Lincoln looked the other way out of policy.

While the Confederate Congress tried to restrict the export of cotton to the North, it never outlawed trade with states remaining in the Union. It was silent on the matter of imports because the necessities of life were often more readily available to Southern civilians on the far side of enemy lines than through the blockade.[14] The regulations of Lincoln's government were more convoluted because of conflicting interests. Prohibition on trade would leave destitute whites and former slaves in federally occupied regions of the Confederate states with no means of economic support. But less altruistically, New England mills wanted feedstock to keep their factories running and workers employed. For diplomatic reasons,

Lincoln wanted enough cotton to slip out of the country to avoid a cotton famine in Europe that might otherwise provoke Old World intervention in the American war.[15]

The first opportunity for the North to secure significant quantities of cotton materialized about six months after the opening shots at Fort Sumter on April 12, 1861. In November 1861, a combined federal navy and army force occupied the Sea Islands near Port Royal, South Carolina. The area was famous for copious production of long-staple Sea Island cotton. Chapter 3 describes the Port Royal Experiment, which used former slaves from among the ten thousand who remained behind after the occupation to raise cotton. It was hoped the ex-slaves could be more productively employed as free laborers on cotton plantations managed by capitalistic Northerners. Although not sufficiently productive to suppress interbelligerent trade, the Port Royal Experiment was followed by similar undertakings promoted by Northern civilians that might enable them to occupy and operate similar plantations in other parts of the Confederacy. Textile mogul Edward Atkinson advocated Texas as a target, while wealthy abolitionist and fellow Massachusetts resident Eli Thayer favored Florida.[16] Such advocacy was partly responsible for later military adventures, such as Louisiana's Red River expedition and Florida's Olustee campaign.[17]

Following the occupation of Port Royal, the next surge of intersectional trade developed in Matamoros, Mexico. Chapter 4 explains how shippers from the Northern states used the legal loophole in the federal blockade noted earlier to circumvent the prohibition against selling contraband to the enemy. They merely pretended their cargoes were destined for Mexico, whereas they were actually used to supply the Confederacy. The chapter also investigates the states' rights policies of Mexico that made such trade possible against the will—for a time—of the central government in Mexico City.[18]

Chapter 5 is devoted to the surge of intersectional trade that grew after Memphis and New Orleans were captured by Union forces just before summer 1862. Both cities were near the center of the world's richest cotton-growing lands. General Butler assumed command in New Orleans, where he was a forceful proponent of trading with the enemy, partly because he was the biggest shareholder in one of the largest textile mills in Massachusetts.[19]

Contrary to popular belief, cargoes entering the Confederacy through the blockade were not necessarily from Europe.[20] Although about twice as much cotton reached the North across enemy lines as was shipped to Europe through the maritime blockade, it is important to realize that some merchants in the Northern states also traded through the blockade.[21] Chapter 6 describes a variety of evasions used. One method was to first ship cargoes to Halifax, Nova Scotia, where they could be converted into "Canadian" merchandise prior to running the blockade. On return, Confederate bales could be transformed into "Canadian cotton" at Halifax and then shipped to New York or other northeastern ports.[22]

After Butler established a reputation as the maestro of wartime intersectional trade in New Orleans, he transferred his aptitudes to Norfolk, Virginia, where he was given command of the occupied port in November 1863. Chapter 7 describes how he once again utilized family members and associates from his New Orleans days to promote trade across enemy lines. In the final months of the war, following the Union capture of the South's last major blockade-running port at Wilmington, North Carolina, Confederate General in Chief Robert E. Lee's besieged army at Petersburg received most of the vital supplies from Butler-controlled Norfolk.[23]

After the fall of the Confederate fortress at Vicksburg, Mississippi, in summer 1863, Rebel states west of the Mississippi River were isolated. Since Union gunboats patrolled the river, it was almost impossible to relocate a Rebel army from one side to the other. It was even difficult to transfer a modest amount of supplies across it, and the Union blockade curtailed transport across the Gulf of Mexico. Consequently, the Confederate Trans-Mississippi Department became almost a nation unto itself. With headquarters in Shreveport, Louisiana, Lieutenant General Edmund Kirby Smith was not only the ultimate military authority for the vast region, but he also controlled important aspects of civilian life. Chapter 8 clarifies how the Confederate Trans-Mississippi figured simultaneously into French ambitions in North America and a free-for-all of intersectional trade as a result of the region's inability to obtain adequate supplies by any other means.[24]

Chapter 9 tells how Lincoln threw wide open the gates of wartime intersectional commerce in the final year of the war. During the second half of 1864, efforts by Congress and the military to throttle such trade put a strain on the Treasury's gold reserves. The president believed that one way to slow the drain was to require that cotton be purchased only with greenback currency (US Treasury notes), which was not backed by gold. When cotton was purchased for gold or specie, the currency would inevitably find its way to international markets, where it would be used to purchase munitions and weapons for the Confederacy. Conversely, when Northerners bought cotton with greenbacks, no specie was transferred to the South. Additionally, cotton obtained with Treasury notes might optionally be exported to Europe in exchange for goods, specie, or gold bullion. Finally, Lincoln believed that a proliferation of greenbacks in the South would provide a powerful economic incentive among residents to favor reunification with the North.[25]

Among the points summarized in the conclusion are that the Confederacy benefitted more from interbelligerent trade than did the North and that the practice lengthened the war.[26] While there were admittedly some altruistic and diplomatically acceptable reasons for Northerners to engage in such trade, the chief motivation was the mercenary gain to be derived from its extraordinary profitability. During the war, cotton prices climbed as high as $1.90 per pound, compared to about 13 cents prior to the war. For those willing to set aside morality in exchange for personal economic advantage, the profits were irresistible, particularly when favored access to available inventories could be secured by means of political connections, bribery, or military status.[27] Efforts to stop it were as futile as King Canute's command to hold back the waves.[28] Historian Merton Coulter concluded, "Business morality reached a very low ebb."[29]

Investigation of the reasons for the North's decision to fight in order to prevent disunion reveals the central explanation for persistence of interbelligerent trade. While a calling to fight for "preservation of the Union" is noble sounding, like most belligerent motivations it is grounded in economics. Specifically, a truncated Northern Union would continue to need cotton feedstock and the South's export engine in order to sustain economic success. In short, it required Southern trade in order to prosper. That is why such commerce continued even across battle lines.

"The levee at Memphis, Tenn.—Hauling sugar and cotton from their hiding-places for shipment north." (*Library of Congress*)

*One*

# The World Cotton Economy

TRADING WITH THE ENEMY WOULD HAVE BEEN IMMATERIAL during the Civil War but for the significance of cotton.

Although the South was desperate for supplies of all kinds, the North had no reason to provide them if the South had nothing of value to trade. While the South's "King Cotton Diplomacy" failed to create enough anxiety in Europe about a war-induced cotton shortage to prompt Great Britain and France to intervene on the side of the Confederacy, the resultant intersectional trade between North and South demonstrated that cotton was no puppet monarch. The Northern states, and the industrialized economies of Europe, were more dependent on the staple than is commonly realized today. The profits were so extraordinarily tempting that efforts to block such trade were hopeless. Historian Lauriston Bullard wrote, "Massachusetts depended almost as much on cotton as did South Carolina and Mississippi."[1] Charles Francis Adams Jr., who was the son of Lincoln's minister to Great Britain and grandson and great-grandson of two American presidents, said, "Boston . . . became . . . a proslavery community, and it remained so until 1861."[2]

King Cotton was not the impotent power it is often ridiculed to be by twenty-first century observers. Ward Hill Lamon, who was one of Lincoln's legal partners for five years before the war and his personal bodyguard during the presidency, explained why Southern secession was such a frightening threat to Northerners:

> [Cotton] formed the bulk of our exchanges with Europe; paid our foreign indebtedness; maintained a great marine; built towns, cities, and railways; enriched factors, brokers, and bankers; filled the federal treasury to overflowing, and made the foremost nations of the world commercially our tributaries and politically our dependents. A short crop embarrassed and distressed all Western Europe; a total failure, a war, or non-intercourse, would reduce whole communities to famine, and probably precipitate them into revolution.[3]

Presently it is easy to take the abundance of cotton clothing for granted. However, in the eighteenth century, cotton was more expensive than wool, linen, or silk. Before mechanization of the cotton textile industry, it took up to fourteen man-days to create one pound of thread, compared to six man-days for silk and two-man days for wool. Like modern semiconductors, from 1784 to the start of the Civil War in 1861, the price of cotton dropped 90 percent owing largely to technological advances in the production process. In response, cotton fabrics rapidly gained market share. In Europe during the century from 1783 to 1883, the fabric rose from a 6 percent share to nearly an 80 percent share, while wool dropped from about 80 percent to 20 percent.[4]

The steadily declining cost created an almost insatiable demand for more cotton. It became known as a cash crop because it was nearly imperishable and could be inventoried indefinitely. It was practically a substitute for gold in international settlements between the United States and Europe. Financiers could extend credit on cotton inventories because it was fungible. In the sixty years from 1801 to 1861, shipping tonnage at Liverpool increased tenfold, from five hundred thousand to five million, translating to a 4 percent growth rate compounded annually.[5] Consequently, cotton textiles became Great Britain's single largest industry at the start of the American Civil War, with about 20 to 25 percent of its population dependent on the sector.[6]

During the seventy-five years prior to the Civil War, the American South became the world's dominant supplier of cotton. Cultivation required long growing seasons providing 180 to 200 frost-free days above sixty degrees Fahrenheit. The crop was typically planted in April or May. When the seeds sprouted in a couple of months, they had to be protected by hand chopping nearby weeds with a hoe. Next came cotton flowers, which burst into bolls in August. The bolls were handpicked through autumn. Before the cotton gin was invented in 1793, seed from the bolls had to be removed by hand. Less than six months after applying for a patent on his gin that mechanized the removal of cottonseeds, Eli Whitney learned that President George Washington granted approval. Unfortunately for Whitney, the government denied his requested renewal eighteen years later. The last step to market was to pack the seed-free cotton into bales typically weighing four hundred to five hundred pounds.[7]

The cotton gin was merely the first in a string of production-process improvements. Examples include water-powered looms, spinning Jennies, and the steam engine. Cotton textile production was the first example of a large-scale industry resulting from the integration of a variety of technological advances.

In 1800, Great Britain imported sixteen million pounds of cotton from the United States, which represented 28 percent of its requirements. By 1860, it was importing 1.23 billion pounds from America, which represented 88 percent of its needs. The British made several attempts to reduce their dependence on Southern cotton, but none were successful. India was a potential alternate supplier. But subcontinent cotton produced 20 percent less yarn and was more difficult to spin, and transportation costs were higher since India lacked railroads and an abundance of navigable rivers. Repeated attempts to reduce dependence on the Southern states consistently failed. For example, efforts to increase annual supplies from India resulted in a gain of only twenty thousand bales from 1800 to 1860, rising from one hundred thousand bales to one hundred twenty thousand.[8] In 1860, the American South produced two-thirds of the world's supply, while Britain accounted for over half of world consumption.[9]

Although New England's textile industry was far smaller than Britain's, it was virtually tied with France for second place. Later, New Englanders made significant improvements on Whitney's gin design, and the region had a number of streams that could be used to power water wheels for mechanized production. Massachusetts became the center of America's textile industry and also the largest manufacturer of cotton gins. As in Britain, on the eve of the Civil War, cotton textiles was America's single biggest industry. In 1860, its goods were valued at $115 million, compared about $73 million for wool and iron, which were the number two and three manufacturing industries respectively.[10]

Northern states were linked to the cotton economy in other ways as well. Although the crop was raised in the South, nearly all the shippers exporting it to Europe were in the New England or middle-Atlantic states. Characteristically, coastal steamers would arrive in Southern ports from New York to discharge imports and load cotton for the return trip to New York, where the cargoes would be reloaded onto transoceanic vessels for export to Europe. Additionally, the lengthy growing season required that the plantation business have ready access to seasonal loans. But there were few banks in the South. Consequently, New York became both a financial and trading center.

At the brink of the Civil War, New York City nearly monopolized international trade in the United States. Tariffs on imports accounted for nearly all of federal tax revenues, and New York City collected two-thirds of the total. When the South's cotton exports passed through the city, New York merchants took as much as 40 percent of the price paid by Europeans for profit and services such as warehousing, shipping, and insurance. As the first Southern states started seceding, New York business leaders became so alarmed that the city's mayor, Fernando Wood, proposed that

Manhattan become an independent city-state similar to the seaport free cities of northern Germany. Wood fantasized about converting New York into a free city with minimal import duties that could supply both the North and South.[11]

Of the original thirteen US colonies, only Georgia and South Carolina became important cotton producers. The real growth came from expansion into the states of Alabama, Mississippi, Louisiana, Arkansas, and Texas. Such states became known as the Old Southwest before the more arid lands farther west took on the identity commonly applied today. Lands in the Old Southwest were cheaper, provided fertile soil, and had good rainfall and a sufficiently long growing season. They were also laced with navigable rivers to provide inexpensive transportation.[12]

Lands in the Old Southwest were auctioned in a mad scramble. Money poured in from the Northern states and Europe. Major buyers included companies with names like New York and Mississippi Land; Boston and New York Chickasaw Land; New York, Mississippi, and Arkansas Land; and Boston and Mississippi Cotton Land. Few of the companies intended to settle and develop the properties. Instead they were speculators who hoped to promptly resell them. It was an orgy of land speculation fueled by an expectation for an ever-rising demand for cotton.[13]

Without cotton, slavery was headed for extinction. It expanded chiefly into regions where cotton could grow, which was principally the Old Southwest. Slavery was considered indispensible for growing and harvesting the labor-intensive crop. But it was also important that slaves could be financed.

Thus, planters used borrowed money to leverage their financial return in a manner similar to wealth accumulated by the World War II generation in America's housing market during the second half of the twentieth century. Rising prices and the financial leverage of a home mortgage enabled many twentieth century homeowners to move into steadily bigger houses as their families grew and to cash out at retirement. The key was to liquidate such properties before a real estate crash.

The situation was much the same for cotton planters. Their plantations became increasingly valuable as cotton production increased. However, since the profits were perpetually reinvested in slave ownership, the planter's wealth fluctuated with the price of slaves. Under such circumstances, uncompensated emancipation meant financial ruin to the owners. Similarly, a halt in geographic expansion would probably lead to a decline in slave prices owing to a steadily rising slave population. On paper, slaves accounted for as much as 60 percent of the South's wealth, with an estimated value of $2 billion to $4 billion for its four million slaves.[14]

So much money was tied up in slave ownership that the South had a shortage of funds for other investments. For example, from 1845 to 1860, banking assets in the South barely increased, from $62 million to $64 million. Meanwhile, bank assets in the North grew from $88 million to $193 million. Thus, the percent of bank assets in the South dropped from 41 percent to 25 percent of the national total in fifteen years. Yet the South was responsible for most of the country's exports. In 1860, Northern exports were only $45 million (20 percent), compared to $193 million (80 percent) in the South, of which $161 million was cotton.[15] Southern exports enabled the United States to maintain a favorable trade balance. Given that gold was the international settlements standard, the country's ability to accumulate reserves was dependent on cotton exports. Cotton exports gave the United States substantial foreign exchange with which to pay for imported goods.

As the South increasingly focused on producing cotton, it had to purchase services from the Northeast, food from the Northwest, and manufactured items from various Northern states. Domestic intersectional trade expanded as cotton exports grew. The Northwest annually sold about $30 million worth of food to Southern cotton producers, who also purchased about $150 million worth of manufactured goods from the North yearly.[16] New England shippers transported cotton to Europe and returned with manufactured goods for Southern consumers. The region's financiers and merchants also found growing demand for their markets in the South. The interregional specialization prompted by slave-grown cotton facilitated public works on waterways and an ever-growing market for New England's cotton textile industry defended by the nation's protective tariffs.[17]

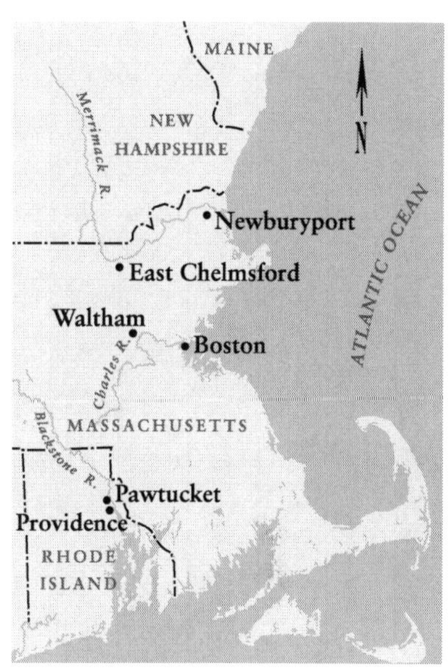

New England Textile Mills.

New England's textile mills were central to America's Industrial Revolution. In 1816, less than 1 percent of the people in the region were employed in manufacturing. Twenty-four years later, in 1840, the figure was nearly 15 percent. The growth was mostly due to cotton textiles. In the late 1830s, two-thirds of the value added in New England manufacturing was in cotton textiles. Industrial use of cotton grew from 5 million pounds in 1790 to 433 million in 1860—more than eight times as fast as domestic population growth.[18]

The region's specialization started as a reaction to the British blockade imposed during the War of 1812. Prior to the conflict, New England's was primarily a maritime economy. By 1805, the United States was the largest carrier of goods from European ports, and one-third of the fleet was in Massachusetts. In Boston harbor alone, the British blockade idled 250 ships. But the blockade also cut off most manufactured goods to the rest of the country. New Englanders foresaw an opportunity to meet the latent demand throughout the country for previously imported consumer goods by becoming a manufacturing center. Consequently, the region's investors poured capital into manufacturing sectors—particularly textiles—in preference to lending money to the federal government.[19]

Francis Cabot Lowell was a brilliant mathematician and Harvard graduate from a wealthy family. On an 1810 trip to Great Britain, he secretly examined the country's textile manufacturing equipment and returned to the United States to copy and improve it. In a stunning incident of industrial piracy, he set up the Boston

Manufacturing Company at Waltham, where he used the Charles River to power waterwheels. It was the first integrated mill turning out cloth from raw cotton. Such was the beginning of the famous Boston Associates that would include the Amory, Cabot, Higginson, Jackson, Russell, Lawrence, and Lee families. Later the families were labeled Boston Brahmins for the highest Hindu caste. The prestige of exclusive Brahmin society ultimately prompted "The Boston Toast":

> And this is good old Boston
> The home of the bean and the cod
> Where the Lowells talk only to the Cabots
> And the Cabots talk only to God[20]

The transition from small-scale operators to power-loom manufacturers led to steadily declining cotton cloth prices that fueled demand. Cotton cloth dropped from 30 cents per yard in 1816, to 6.5 cents in 1843.[21] Historian Ronald Bailey concluded:

> New England graduated from shipping southern cotton to Europe and importing European manufactures . . . for distribution in the USA, to manufacturing these goods for the domestic markets. . . . Southern purchases of cotton goods from U.S. producers amounted to $27 million for the year ended June 30, 1860. This was about one-third of the total output of New England's cotton textile industry for the period. . . . The combination of . . . increasing incomes from raw cotton exports to Europe, expansion of commercial and manufacturing activities in New England and rapid . . . settlement of the West gave rise to sustained growth . . . for New England's cotton textile industry for many decades. . . . New England became the most rapidly expanding market for southern cotton. . . . In this way southern dependence moved from Britain to New England, to the great advantage of the latter's commerce and industry, especially the cotton textile industry.[22]

By the mid-1830s, industrial New England had become wedded to the institution of slavery. It depended on a steady flow of cotton for profits. Northern bankers grew rich providing credit to Southern planters. The Northern maritime industry eagerly anticipated annual growth in cotton exports. Consequently, the economic interests of the disparate regions drew their leaders into tolerant and cordial relations.

For example, among the Brahmins, a youthful Amos Adams Lawrence was sent by his father (Amos Lawrence) to tour the South as an agent for various Boston firms to spread goodwill among the planters. He was welcomed enthusiastically everywhere from Louisville to New Orleans to Mobile to Charleston. In return, Southern planters vacationed in New England summer resorts where they mixed with Northern manufacturers in Saratoga, New York, and Newport, Rhode Island. Each developed a tolerant regard for the rights of the other, cemented by personal friendships that strengthened economic ties.

Conservative Northerners were repelled as abolitionism began to take root about the same time. They shuddered with horror when abolitionists criticized the US Constitution by proclaiming that any compact with slavery was evil and such a Union should be dissolved. Amos Lawrence, whose last name would later be taken by an abolitionist town in Kansas much hated by Missouri bushwhackers, told Robert Rhett of South Carolina that he would never interfere in the matter "unless requested by my brethren in the slaveholding states." The New England cotton aristocracy, which was politically aligned with the Whigs, sought to reassure its Southern friends that abolitionists were merely a lunatic fringe not to be taken seriously. Abolitionist William Lloyd Garrison was booked for his own protection as a "rioter" by Boston police when one of his speeches was interrupted by an angry mob in 1835.[23]

Feelings against abolitionists were even stronger in New York. Five days before South Carolina seceded in December 1860, the Union Committee of Fifteen organized a meeting of business leaders in the Wall Street district to advocate for maintenance of the Union and to show support for Southern grievances. Two hundred were invited, but two thousand showed up. Among them were former president Millard Fillmore, Rothschild banking representative August Belmont, aristocrat William Astor, and future presidential candidate Samuel J. Tilden. Major cotton merchant Richard Lathers led the group. He began by directing his comments to Southern planters to "consider their duties to that part of their Northern brethren whose sympathies have always been with Southern rights and against Northern aggression."[24]

Also attending was John Dix, who would later become a Union general deeply involved in interbelligerent trade and still later governor of New York. Dix also publicly addressed the cotton states by adding, "We will not review the dark history of the aggression and insult visited upon you by Abolitionists and their abettors during the last 35 years. Our detestation of these acts of hostility is not inferior to your own."[25]

Three weeks later, New York mayor Wood spoke to the city's governing Common Council of his stunning proposal that the city join the tide of sentiment triggered by South Carolina and secede to become an independent city-state. "With our aggrieved brethren of the Slave States we have friendly relations and common sympathy. . . . An [independent New York City] would have the whole and united support of the Southern States as well as all other states to whose interests and rights under the constitution she has always been true."[26] Forty years earlier, cotton became the country's chief export. During the ensuing four decades, New York City grew to become the nation's commercial and financial center largely because of its primacy in the cotton trade.

New York started with a natural advantage that it was the only port on the East Coast that was deep enough to handle the largest ships of the era at any tide. By 1818, the city offered scheduled service across the Atlantic to and from Liverpool with the launch of the Black Ball Line. The line's ships were commonly referred to as "packets" because they regularly delivered pouches of postal and diplomatic mail. Packet ships would carry imports from Great Britain to New York and thence down the Eastern Seaboard to Southern ports such as Charleston and Savannah, and ultimately to gulf ports such as New Orleans and Mobile. On the return trips, their holds would be full of cotton. Only four years after the formation of the Black Ball Line, cotton accounted for 40 percent of New York's exports. By 1825, the city's port status was enhanced with completion of the Erie Canal, which opened trade with the rapidly growing Great Lakes states.[27]

Nonetheless, abolitionists gained traction in the North from 1835 to 1857. Even "Cotton Whigs"—Northern Whigs such as the Boston Brahmins with political and economic links to Southern planters—concluded that slavery should not be permitted to expand into additional states as western territories were admitted into the Union. However, they did not change viewpoints so far as to abandon support for the constitutional right of slavery to remain as a state's right among those states where it was already legal. One trigger was the 1854 Kansas-Nebraska Act, which adopted the doctrine of "popular sovereignty." Specifically the act mandated that the slave or free status of future states from the Kansas and Nebraska territories would be determined by a popular vote of their citizens. Selected Cotton Whigs, such as Amos A. Lawrence, provided funding to help nonslaveholders settle in Kansas, and it was for him that the town of Lawrence was named.[28] As a result, the territory became a center of encounters between pro-slavery and anti-slavery settlers. As such confrontations escalated into persistent violence, the situation was labeled "Bleeding Kansas." The Kansas violence was symptomatic of the flammable differences between North and South that Senator William H. Seward of New York predicted would erupt in an "irrepressible conflict" of civil war involving the entire country.

But the financial Panic of 1857 prompted Cotton Whigs to refocus on strengthening ties to the South, which remained relatively prosperous. Southerners threatened to boycott manufactured goods from the North and to instead rely on imports. Planters wanted a new deal from the Northern moneychangers, who they felt were extracting too much of the value of cotton for their services. Northerners became even more alarmed in March 1858, when Senator John Hammond of South Carolina delivered his "King

Cotton" speech, which included the rhetorical question of what would happen if "no cotton was furnished [to the North] for three years?" In response, the *New York Herald* wrote, "the people must forget about Bleeding Kansas." The *Boston Post* added that the dogma of an "irrepressible conflict" must be "vot(ed) down."

Cotton Whigs concluded that Republicans were a dangerous sectional party whose aims could only lead to disunion and disaster. Searching for a way to promote a national party that could appeal to both North and South, the Cotton Whigs first leaned toward the anti-Catholic and anti-Irish Know-Nothings' American Party. But it had little appeal in the South. Shortly before the 1860 presidential election, the Constitutional Union Party was formed in Boston. John Bell of Tennessee became its presidential candidate and former Cotton Whig Edward Everett of Massachusetts was the vice presidential nominee. The party professed to the simple political principles of the Constitution and the Union of states. It hoped to avoid disunion by taking no stand on slavery.[29]

TABLE 1

| Southern Cotton Production | | 1860 Cotton Consumption | |
|---|---|---|---|
| Year | Bales (1000s) | Country | Bales (1000s) |
| 1861 | 4,500 | Great Britain | 2,633 |
| 1862 | 1,500 | United States | 650 |
| 1863 | 450 | France | 621 |
| 1864 | 300 | Russia | 325 |
| | | Germany | 307 |

Source: Owsley, Frank. *King Cotton Diplomacy.* (University of Chicago Press, 1931)

As Table 1 shows, Great Britain was by far the world's biggest cotton consumer, with the United States ranking a distant second. British textile companies exported fabric throughout the world, including the United States. They even reexported raw cotton.

As a means of motivating Great Britain and France to intervene on behalf of the Confederacy, shortly after the war began in 1861,

Southerners initiated an unofficial embargo of cotton exports and a drop in cotton plantings. The strategy became known as King Cotton Diplomacy. Since about one-fourth of the British population was economically dependent on the cotton textile industry, Britain's ability to abide the economic consequences of the war would depend on the length of the conflict and the country's available inventory of raw cotton and finished textile goods.

Much of the decline in cotton production, from 4.5 million bales in 1861 to 300,000 bales in 1864, reflected King Cotton policies, in addition to disruptions resulting from invading Union armies. First, at the start of the war, Southerners hoped that intentional and deep reductions in planted cotton acreage would convince Great Britain and France that the embargo was more than temporary, thereby implying that the world could face long-term cotton starvation if the Civil War became protracted. Second, in place of cotton, Southerners resolved to grow more of their own food because the northwestern states would no longer be reliable sources of provender during wartime.[30]

TABLE 2

Cotton Prices Per Pound in New York and Liverpool, 1860–1865

| | New York (Cents) | | | Liverpool (Pence) | | |
|---|---|---|---|---|---|---|
| Season | Low | High | Avg. | Low | High | Avg. |
| 1860–61 | 10 | 22 | 13 | 7 | 12 | 9 |
| 1861–62 | 20 | 52 | 31 | 12 | 29 | 18 |
| 1862–63 | 51 | 92 | 67 | 20 | 29 | 22 |
| 1863–64 | 68 | 189 | 102 | 22 | 31 | 27 |
| 1864–65 | 35 | 182 | 83 | 13 | 26 | 19 |

Source: Watkins, James L. *King Cotton.* (New York, 1908, p. 30)
Rounded to the nearest whole number.

As Table 2 illustrates, cotton prices sharply increased during the war, initially because of the embargo and later as a result of a progressively more effective blockade. During summer 1864, the New York price rose to almost $1.90 a pound; the Liverpool price climbed as high as thirty-one pence (there were 240 pence in each pound sterling). Before and after the war, thirty-one pence equaled about sixty-three cents. However, as a result of the drain on the North's and South's gold reserves caused by massive war-induced imports, both Confederate currency and the US greenback dollar depreciated considerably in relation to sterling. For example, before the war, each pound sterling was worth $4.77 in US currency, whereas at the end of the war, it converted to about $7.90 in greenbacks.[31]

When the war began, Britain had about 2.3 million bales warehoused from the Southern states, aside from a large amount of Asian cotton. Britain started the war with sizable finished-goods inventories as well. Partly because of a decline in demand from the Southern states, Britain's cotton textile export market initially shrank. In short, finished goods were overstocked for a year or so. Consequently, textile industry executives originally welcomed the higher prices prompted by the war because the inflation provided substantial inventory profits. "In place of hard times, they had a shower of riches."[32]

When the war began, the stage was set for a showdown between King Cotton and the untested ability of Europe's economies to diversify into other profitable industries. Unless the economic foundations of Great Britain and New England were to change radically within a couple of years, both regions were likely to experience economic hardship without cotton. As shall be discovered, the Northern textile industry would grab most of the Southern supply by trading with the enemy. Despite the risk that a "cotton famine" in Europe might prompt Britain and France to intervene on the side of the Confederacy, domestic textile makers prioritized their own needs. Although Northern cotton mill consumption dropped about 60 percent during the war, higher prices for finished goods enabled mill owners to prosper. Massachusetts textile mogul Amos A. Lawrence wrote at the height of the war that his business was "better than ever." He was particularly gratified that there was "no dickering about prices and almost all sales were for cash."[33]

*Two*

# Official Policy

OFFICIAL POLICY TOWARD INTERBELLIGERENT TRADE IN THE Confederacy and the United States evolved fitfully. Ultimately it became a matter of necessity for the Rebels, whereas it was a matter of policy for Lincoln's government.

## CONFEDERACY

The Confederate Congress never outlawed trade with the United States but instead attempted to regulate it. Less than a month after the opening shots at Fort Sumter, a congressional committee investigated the merits of a prohibition of cotton exports to the North while limiting imports to munitions and food. No such proposition was ever enacted. Instead, in May and August 1861, Congress passed laws restricting specific exports such as cotton, tobacco, and sugar to Confederate seaports, or across the Mexican border. The stipulations had the effect of prohibiting shipment of the enumerated items to the Northern states. Conversely, the laws were silent about imports, thereby permitting Southerners to purchase merchandise, including the necessities of war, from the United States.[1]

Prior to secession, nearly all manufactured goods required in the South were either imported or purchased from Northern states. Only a small fraction arrived directly from Europe. Generally, overseas merchandise arrived first in New York and was thereafter shipped by railroad, inland waterways, or coastal steamers to the Southern states. Ships coming into the region from foreign ports typically arrived in ballast to pick up cotton. Less than two weeks after Sumter, Lincoln declared a blockade of Southern ports from Virginia to Texas.[2]

Ironically, the Confederate cotton embargo was half-consistent with Lincoln's blockade policy. As a result, the chief blockade consequence to Southerners was a limitation on imports. Confederate analysts estimated a "cotton famine" would materialize in Europe by February or March 1862. But by spring 1862, Europe's cotton shortage was less intense than the Confederacy's need for imports and international monetary credits. Consequently, voluntary embargo compliance disintegrated because cotton was the only practical means of obtaining needed goods and establishing credit abroad.

In order to prevent valuable Southern commodities from falling into Union hands, a bill enacted in April 1862 prohibited exports through any Confederate location occupied by federal soldiers, but there continued to be no restriction on imports. The following month, Congress passed a bill requiring the destruction of most crops, including cotton, when there was the slightest danger of it falling into enemy hands.[3]

Confederate armies were primarily supplied through three organizations. First was the Commissary Department. Commissary General Lucius Northrop directed the department until being replaced in February 1865 by Isaac St. John. Their job was to supply provender. Second was the quartermaster general, who was responsible for obtaining clothing and similar items such as saddles. Abraham Myers occupied the post until succeeded by Alexander Lawton in August 1863. Finally, the Bureau of Ordnance supplied munitions and weapons and was supervised by Josiah Gorgas during the entire war. He entered the post as a major and ended a brigadier general.

Four months after the opening guns at Fort Sumter, Commissary General Northrop realized there were not enough hogs in the

Confederacy to meet military needs and the beef in Texas would be hard to transport to the principal armies. By January 1862, he concluded that interbelligerent trade would be necessary. "On commencing the organization in Montgomery it was known that supplies, especially of salt meats, could not be obtained to an adequate extent except in the enemy's country. Accordingly, appropriate steps were taken to reach them. The stores of bacon and pork thus acquired, at a cost to the Government of much less than one-half of the current rates, are still being issued."[4]

By October 1862, Secretary of War George Randolph endorsed intersectional trade as a necessity when a Memphis resident arrived in the Confederate capital of Richmond, Virginia, proposing to sell large amounts of provisions in exchange for cotton located behind Rebel lines. (Federal troops occupied Memphis in June 1862 and continued to hold it until the end of the war.) Randolph recommended the transaction to President Davis, arguing that the prohibition of cotton exports through enemy-occupied cities only applied to citizens and not the Confederate government.[5]

Davis was cool to the idea. When he suggested that the transaction be delayed, Randolph resigned. His successor, James Seddon, soon adopted an attitude similar to Randolph's. He told military authorities that they need not arrest Northern traders who came through the lines unless they were suspected of spying. Since Northrop stated plainly that he could not adequately supply Confederate armies with required provender unless he was permitted to trade cotton across those lines, Davis subordinates gradually adopted a "don't ask, don't tell" strategy toward the president. Intersectional trade continued to grow.[6] For example, in spring 1863, Seddon wrote to General Joseph Johnston in Tennessee, encouraging the general to "obtain within your own department or the well stocked counties of Kentucky [behind enemy lines] all possible supplies. I am informed that you could probably obtain considerable supplies from Kentucky if you felt authorized to trade cotton or sugar for meat."[7]

By the end of 1862, Commissary General Northrop advocated impressment, but Congress resisted. Therefore, by indirect hints here and there, he encouraged army commanders to unilaterally impress whatever supplies they needed from nearby civilians in order to motivate congressional action. Virtually all except Robert E. Lee's Army of Northern Virginia complied. Consequently, during winter and spring 1863, Lee could not concentrate his full army along the Rappahannock River defense line. Lieutenant General James Longstreet's corps was temporarily relocated to southeast Virginia and northeast North Carolina, where more supplies were available. As a result, when Union Major General Joseph Hooker crossed the Rappahannock to attack Lee, Longstreet's corps was too distant to help, and the Confederates were outnumbered two-to-one, although Lee and his other corps commander, Thomas "Stonewall" Jackson, still managed to beat Hooker at the battle of Chancellorsville. Despite the relocation of Longstreet's corps, the incremental supplies endemically located in its district were not enough to offset a chronic shortage. Consequently, during that period, both corps of Lee's army were partly supplied by trading across enemy lines.[8]

By late March 1863, Congress passed an impressment law. The following month it passed a tax bill that included a provision for tithing-in-kind. Every farmer was to reserve a fixed amount of produce for family needs and then deliver one-tenth of the excess to the government in a marketable condition. The terms also applied to salted pork, although beeves were taxed as income.[9]

Standing orders to burn cotton rather than let invading Union armies capture it were often enforced by torch-carrying Confederate cavalrymen. If there was no opportunity to sell crops and inventories, planters acquiesced, or even eagerly participated in the conflagrations. However, Northern traders quickly learned that if they could get behind Confederate lines ahead of advancing Union armies, they could induce planters to sell cotton rather than burn it. Such was the underlying dynamic for most of the intersectional trade during the war; Northern traders provided the primary incentive that deterred Southerners from destroying cotton.[10] When the incentive was absent, Southerners deliberately burned an estimated 2.5 million bales during the war.[11] The 1863 annual report for the Boston Board of Trade stated, "The Confederates have guarded [cotton] with unusual vigilance burning . . . all likely to fall into our hands, knowing that the 'Cotton Famine' [is the best way] of bringing about recognition of their confederacy."[12]

Confederate General Richard Taylor, who commanded various armies in some of the richest cotton lands, including Louisiana, Mississippi, and Alabama, confirmed how the monetary incentive combined with basic human needs could lead Rebel officers to ignore orders to burn cotton:

> Outpost officers would violate the law and trade. In vain they were removed; the temptation was too strong and their successors did the same. The influence upon the women was dreadful, and in many cases their appeals were heart rendering. Mothers with suffering children whose husbands were already in the War or already fallen would beseech me for permits to take cotton through the lines. It was useless to explain that it was against the law. . . . This did not give food and clothing to their children.[13]

On February 6, 1864, Congress enacted a law granting the government more power to trade with the United States but restricting the terms of such trade for private citizens. Specifically, residents were prohibited from accepting greenbacks in any transaction, whereas the Confederate government was allowed to do so. Private citizens who sold cotton were required to accept gold, specie, or Confederate currency, or to barter. Consequently, the government began to account for a growing share of commerce with Northern traders.[14] By the end of the year, Commissary General Northrop stated that while it was difficult to persuade, or force, Southerners to sell goods to the commissary, interbelligerent trade had been "successful beyond expectations" in obtaining provender from enemy-held territory. He cited an example of trading a pound of cotton for a pound of bacon.

A secret act of February 18, 1865, enabled the secretary of the Treasury to selectively grant private exporters exemptions to such restrictions, with the result that between-the-lines trading became increasingly liberal in the final months of the war. Essentially, both the Confederate government and licensed exporters were authorized to sell goods for greenbacks if nothing better, such as gold, could be obtained from the buyers.[15]

### United States

Owing to conflicting goals within discrete industrial and political circles, interbelligerent trade policy in the North was convoluted, even sometimes contradicting blockade and military objectives. As historian Merton Coulter put it, "The problems that met the United States government in dealing with this question were almost insurmountable. . . . The government vacillated from an intention, announced in the beginning, of completely stopping trade . . . to an almost unrestricted intercourse near the end of the War."[16]

Such trade was undoubtedly harmful from a military viewpoint because it provided the Rebels with arms and other necessities. Together with Secretary of War Edwin Stanton, most military leaders favored outright prohibition. As historian Thomas O'Connor explained the viewpoint:

> Every bale sold meant additional guns and ammunition for the Rebel cause; every transaction spelled additional credit in England for the purchase of ships and supplies . . . [Stanton] maintained that anyone found trading with the enemy should be shot. Agreeing with him were most of the professional army officers. . . . According to this point of view not a single bale of cotton would have been allowed to leave the dockyards or depots of the South until the rebellion had been completely crushed.[17]

When the cotton shortage in Europe was becoming its severest, Lincoln's cabinet met to consider what should be done. Attorney General Edward Bates summarized the legal point favoring the military and supported it during the session: "[T]o trade with the public enemy is to give that enemy aid and comfort—and if that be a crime in the individual it is folly in the Government for which it will be sure . . . to pay the penalty."[18]

Nonetheless, New England textile mills persistently hungered for cotton, and Lincoln was compelled to consider other perspectives. Secretary of State William Seward and Treasury Secretary Salmon Chase each voiced one.

Seward realized that if at least some cotton did not leak through the blockade, a European cotton famine was a genuine threat that could become severe enough to prompt European intervention on the side of the South. As early as July 1862, Senator Orville Browning of Illinois recorded Lincoln as saying, "England wants us to permit her to get $50 million worth of cotton from the South."[19] While Europeans might abide a moderate shortage, acute cotton starvation could threaten their economic and political stability. Such a threshold was approached early in 1863, when some British districts reported 40 percent of their workers unemployed and on relief.[20] The court of Louis-Napoléon Bonaparte (Napoleon III) was particularly apprehensive because older citizens still remembered the Reign of Terror following the French Revolution.[21]

Secretary Chase appreciated that Southern cotton alone accounted for two-thirds of American exports in 1860.[22] The war, and the federal blockade of Southern ports, sharply curtailed those exports. This wasn't just a problem for the textile industry; the Union could not hope for a favorable trade balance without cotton. Given that gold was the international settlements standard, the situation could strain the Treasury, which would erode America's international status and also invite foreign recognition of the Confederacy.

Newspaper editorials from the Northeast underscored such concerns. Lincoln was a regular reader of the *Washington Chronicle*, which noted that the acquisition of cotton in the Northern states would bolster the gold standard and improve American credit overseas. With the largest Civil War era circulation, the *New York Herald* similarly proclaimed, "Our mills need cotton. Every bale of it reduces the price of gold and so sustains the government and mitigates the distress caused by a depreciated currency." The *New York Commercial Advertiser* identified a related factor by observing that Southerners "want money" to buy the necessities of life. "Take their cotton and give them greenbacks and they will speedily feel the force of the old tie" to the Union.[23]

Finally, there was also a humanitarian impulse. Once Union armies occupied parts of the Confederacy, intersectional trade was almost the only way that ex-slaves and destitute whites—including those loyal to the Union—avoided starvation. As a result of the poverty left behind after Confederates withdrew from western Tennessee, Major General Henry Halleck wrote that the cotton trade was a matter of "extreme necessity." A Western Sanitary Commission founder commented, "Hundreds of women and children in this vicinity are in a starving condition." Retreating Confederates had taken everything "even to the last milch cow."[24]

Slaves and former slaves were similarly affected. After reporting that federal troops had confiscated 700 acres of his corn, 150 of his cattle, and 400 of his hogs, a Southern planter sought permission to buy a sizable quantity of bacon to feed the hundred slaves wishing to remain on his plantation. Otherwise he desired to turn them over to federal authorities because he did not want them to starve.[25]

For five months after the formation of the Confederacy in February 1861, Congress imposed no restrictions on intersectional trade. However, a week before the First Battle of Bull Run in July, an act passed prohibiting "commercial intercourse" with the insurrectionary states except as provided by licensed exemptions directed by the president. A month later, Lincoln declared that such permits would be issued through the Treasury Department. Unfortunately, the lucrative profits available in cotton trade inevitably subjected the permitting process to influences of political favoritism that invited bribery and other forms of corruption. Lincoln would later complain that if an intelligent angel were to observe White House conversations, "I think he would come to the conclusion that this war is being prosecuted for [the purpose of] obtaining cotton from the South for Northern cotton mills."[26] Treasury agents were to supervise the activities and were ordered to confer with the generals commanding the applicable departments. However, the agents and licensed traders were only partially responsible to such generals because they reported directly to the Treasury Department.[27]

In May 1862, Congress authorized the Treasury secretary to refuse clearance to ships with cargoes ultimately destined for the

Confederacy, although Secretary Chase had already effectively adopted the policy a year earlier. If suspicious that cargoes headed for neutral destinations such as Nassau were really intended for the Confederacy, US customs officials could require the shipper to post a bond equal to the value of the cargo. The bond was to be refunded when the US consul at the destination port verified that the cargo went to neutral buyers. Unfortunately, bonds were sometimes refunded ("repurchased") with bribery amounting to a small fraction of the bond value, and the "neutral buyers" were often middlemen who sold to blockade-runners.

Secretary of the Treasury Salmon P. Chase. (*Library of Congress*)

Previously a senator from Ohio, Chase was politically ambitious. Many suspected he hoped to win the presidency in 1864. In 1860, he and Seward were the leading traditional contenders at the Republican presidential convention that ultimately selected Lincoln as the party's candidate. As a result of the deficit spending necessitated by the Civil War, Chase promoted a paper currency act that resulted in the issuance of greenbacks as legal tender even though they had no gold backing. In furtherance of his political ambitions, some of the greenback denominations featured his face on the bills. That is one reason why only images of dead people are currently allowed on US currency and postage stamps.

Chase's political ambitions steadily increased tensions with Lincoln. The secretary resented interference from the president and submitted his resignation multiple times before summer 1864, only to have Lincoln decline to accept it. However, after Lincoln secured his party's 1864 presidential nomination, Chase tendered his resignation one too many times, in protest over Lincoln's objection to Chase's selection of a new customs director in New York harbor. The president accepted the resignation. However, toward the end of that year, Lincoln eliminated Chase as a political adversary by appointing him to the Supreme Court, and he became chief justice of the United States.[28]

While managing interbelligerent trade, Chase was never convicted of improprieties, but there were questionable connections, which will be discussed more fully later. During the war his eldest daughter, Kate, married Rhode Island's governor and later US senator, William Sprague. The man owned one of the country's biggest textile mills, with nine plants. As early as spring 1862, Sprague's name was connected with behind-the-lines cotton trading.[29] Chase also appointed a relative named George Denison as a Treasury agent in New Orleans. Although the youth was initially suspicious and vigilant of the commerce involving General Benjamin Butler and his brother, Denison later became a bribe taker.[30] Historian James Ford Rhodes concluded, "Chase was a poor judge of men and made bad appointments."[31]

One of Chase's first biographers from the nineteenth century, Albert Bushnell Hart, summarized the secretary's performance on the matter of wartime intersectional commerce:

> The administration of the Treasury during the war has no more unsavory side than the scramble for permits and the collusion of military officers in getting property from the enemy's lines; yet for no object did the secretary more honestly bestir himself than to regulate the trade. The circumstances were too much for him, as they were for the most upright commanders in the field.[32]

A couple of years after the flaws of the August 1861 regulations became evident, Chase attempted to gain more control over articles entering the rebellious states via overland trade. New regulations were adopted on September 11, 1863, establishing "special agencies" in occupied regions. Within such agencies, authorized private citizens were allowed to operate stores, much like Indian trading posts, enabling nearby residents to buy and sell merchandise. The stores were permitted to sell a limited monthly dollar volume of merchandise to civilians, but they could buy unlimited amounts of whatever residents offered for sale, including cotton. Volume limitations on items sold to Southerners could be inflated by specifying them as "plantation supplies" as opposed to "family supplies." Historian Merton Coulter wrote, "The abuses of the trading stations were so flagrant as to cause an honest person to lose faith in the integrity of his fellow man." One member of an investigating House Commerce Committee said, "If I were to mention the facts, they would make the cheek of every American Senator tingle with shame."[33]

By summer 1864, it was clear that the Treasury practice of issuing permits to individuals for the purpose of trading in cotton was rife with corruption. Congress concluded a better method was to only allow Treasury agents (i.e., government employees) to buy cotton. The agents could then resell the cotton at auctions where the ultimate buyers would presumably be domestic textile makers or firms seeking to export raw cotton overseas. Therefore, on July 2, 1864, Congress passed the Purchasing Act, which withdrew the president's power to issue permits to private citizens.

However, with the cooperation of Treasury Secretary William Fessenden, who had replaced Chase in early July 1864, Lincoln cleverly sidestepped the proscription with a set of Treasury Department implementation rules. Specifically, the September 24, 1864, rules allowed anyone who owned goods behind Confederate lines to bring them into designated federally occupied depot cities and sell them to a Treasury agent. Since "any person whatsoever" could "bring in" merchandise, the stipulations essentially enabled individual Northern traders to continue operating, only in a different manner.

They could (1) infiltrate Confederate lines, (2) buy cotton from the original Rebel owner, even if it was the Confederate government, and (3) bring the purchased items (e.g., cotton, tobacco, turpentine) into a federally occupied depot, where it could be sold to a Treasury agent. Furthermore, the Lincoln-Fessenden rules required that proceeds to the seller be paid in US greenbacks equal to three-fourths of the market price at New York. Although it represented a 25 percent discount, the New York selling price was still far above what was paid behind Rebel lines.

Such rules nullified the intent of the Purchasing Act. In fact, they enabled more independent businessmen to become cotton traders. All that was required was the audacity to infiltrate the frontier, negotiate attractive purchase contracts with the enemy, and transport the acquired goods to a federal depot. While permits to transport cotton would help to physically get it through the lines, unlike the earlier Treasury permits, they did not give the holders a privileged right to trade it. No doubt, bribery was a common means of securing safe infiltration into enemy territory and obtaining access to military wagons, vessels, or railroads to get the cotton to a destination depot. The greenback requirement reflected Lincoln's intention that such trade spread a preference for US paper currency throughout the South, thereby weakening Confederate influence.[34]

Although cotton supplies might be acquired by confiscation, both Lincoln and Congress initially moved cautiously in order to avoid alienating the border states early in the war before they were firmly under Union control. The First Confiscation Act of August 1861 only permitted confiscation of property actively employed to resist federal authority. Thus, slaves and cotton bales used in construction of Rebel fortifications could both be confiscated as contraband. But cotton in the form of baled inventory or crops in the field could not be confiscated. However, the Second Confiscation Act eleven months later permitted the confiscation of any property owned by Confederate citizens, whether they were civilians or soldiers. Thus, under the second act, a planter whose family was in rebellion to federal authority could lose his property—including slaves and cotton—to confiscation.[35]

Another reason the quantities of cotton obtained through confiscation were less than federal authorities hoped was that Northern traders would buy eligible inventories before they could be captured. The traders were so hungry for cotton profits they would even buy confiscation-eligible stocks owned by the Confederate government. Although such stocks were undeniably subject to confiscation, corrupted traders would turn their heads while bales marked "C. S. A" had their marking removed in order to pretend they were owned by holders whose properties could not be legally confiscated, such as Union-loyal citizens. By July 1864, it is estimated that two-thirds of the cotton awaiting shipment north was sold by the Confederate government. By then, the blockade had sufficiently tightened that the Confederacy would sell directly to the enemy and accept US currency as payment.[36]

William P. Fessenden was appointed secretary of the Treasury upon Salmon Chase's resignation in 1864. (*Library of Congress*)

In addition to the Confiscation Acts, Congress passed the Revenue Act of August 6, 1861, which included a direct tax on properties aimed at raising $20 million for the federal government. Each state was assigned a proportionate share of the $20 million based on its population. Financial assets such as stocks and bonds were exempt properties, although real estate and slaves were included in the taxable base. Therefore, the tax was unpopular in states with many small farmers and especially the Union-loyal border states where slavery was legal. Finally, it permitted properties in all states—including those in rebellion—to be seized for nonpayment of taxes, although there was initially no mechanism for collecting the taxes in the insurrectionary states.

Therefore, an act of June 7, 1862, authorized Lincoln to appoint tax commissioners for each Confederate state. The commissioners were empowered to calculate the taxes due on each property within such states that were also within Union occupation lines. Delinquent owners had sixty days to pay the tax, plus a 50 percent penalty. If the tax and penalty were not paid by the deadline, the commissioners could seize the underlying real estate and sell it at auction. Although written as a tax law, it was really a pretext for confiscation that was sometimes even more effective than the First or Second Confiscation Acts.[37]

Because overland intersectional trade was an alternative to maritime blockade-running, it is necessary to examine the legal status of the federal naval blockade. Immediately after the shooting started in

April 1861, Lincoln and Seward sought to block international commerce to Southern states. However, they desired to do so in a manner least likely to inflame tensions with European powers. During discussions with European diplomats in Washington prior to the war's opening shots, Seward came to understand that conformance with the Declaration of Maritime Law, which was a component of the 1856 Treaty of Paris ending the Crimean War, would likely provide the least antagonistic way to block international commerce to Southern ports. Although the United States was not among the fifty-five signatories to the Paris agreement, Great Britain and France were. Therefore, Lincoln and Seward decided to formulate their plans on the declaration, which provided two ways to shut down maritime trade to selected American ports. First was to close the ports, followed by action of US Navy ships to collect duties and penalties on the high seas from neutral vessels violating the closure. Second was a formal blockade.[38]

Initially, Lincoln and Seward preferred the closure option because it avoided an implied recognition that Southern ports were part of a separate nation. However, there were two problems with closing the harbors. First, the Constitution specified that all ports must be treated equally. The president lacked the legal authority to close some and leave others open.[39] Second, Lord Richard Lyons, the British envoy to Washington, had earlier warned Seward that closing the ports was a worse option than a blockade because it increased the probability of a high seas confrontation between a neutral carrier and a US warship. Two days after Sumter surrendered, Lyons wrote to Lord John Russell, the British foreign secretary in London:

> A regular blockade would be less objectionable than . . . closing the Southern Ports. . . . The rules of blockade are to a great extent determined and known. . . . But if the US are to be permitted to seize any ship of ours wherever they can find her within their jurisdiction on the plea that by going to a Southern port she has violated the US customs laws, our commerce will be exposed to vexations beyond bearing. . . . It would certainly jus-

> tify Great Britain and France in recognizing the Southern Confederacy and sending their fleets to force the U.S. to treat British and French vessels as neutrals in conformity with the laws of nations.[40]

By the end of April 1861, the federal government had announced a blockade that would cover all Confederate ports from Virginia to Texas. The British reacted the following month with the Queen's Proclamation of Neutrality, which officially classified the Confederacy as a belligerent, but not a diplomatically recognized country. Thus, Rebel ships in British and colonial ports were thereafter allowed to obtain fuel, supplies, and repairs. The commerce raiders *Alabama, Florida,* and *Shenandoah* were examples of Rebel ships that would utilize such provisions. As a belligerent, the Confederacy was also permitted to buy weapons and supplies from neutral countries. However, Queen Victoria clarified that the 1818 Foreign Enlistments Act, which prohibited British subjects from joining a belligerent navy and signified that any British ship running a blockade did so at its own risk, would also apply to the situation in America. Thus, her government would not seek the release of captured blockade-runners.[41]

Fortunately for the United States, following Great Britain's lead, the other European powers ignored the provision in the Paris declaration specifying that blockades were only legal if they were "effective"—meaning capable of being reliably enforced. For much of the war—certainly the first year or two—the federal blockade failed to be effective because too few ships were available to enforce it dependably. Although Confederate foreign commissioners correctly argued that the blockade did not meet the required standards of legality, Britain and the rest of Europe disregarded their pleas. Thus, blockade-running became a separate business in which European deep water vessels carried cargo to centers like Nassau and Bermuda, where the last leg of the trip into the Confederacy was executed by specialized carriers that assumed the risk of capture.

Britain concealed its chief reason for failing to recognize the illegalities of the blockade. Essentially, it was not merely thinking of the present war in North America but of potential future European conflicts. The Paris declaration had never been popular with leaders whose prime interest was the prominence of the British Empire. It reduced the flexibility of the British fleet to protect its interests. In fact, that was the precise objective of the Continental powers sponsoring the declaration. Essentially, the British could not optimally employ their fleet in a future war if it was required to effectively blockade mile after mile of enemy coastlines, such as, hypothetically, the combined Atlantic and Mediterranean shorelines of France. If signatories of the Paris declaration generally acquiesced to Lincoln's implementation of the blockade, it would become a legal international precedent that would effectively nullify the treaty provisions most objectionable to the British navy.[42]

*Three*

# The Port Royal Experiment

DURING THE FIRST YEAR OF THE CIVIL WAR, A MASSACHUSETTS mill owner, abolitionist, and antebellum weapons supplier to John Brown named Edward Atkinson wrote a booklet titled *Cheap Cotton by Free Labor*. "Free" referred to nonslave white or black workers. "The object of this . . . pamphlet is to prove that labor upon cotton . . . by whites . . . will yield a larger return to the small cultivator than almost any other agricultural product." His book promoted a belief that cotton could be produced at lower cost by eliminating slavery and substituting free laborers. He advocated destruction of the power of the "planters and businessmen of the cities" in order to rebuild the Union with the "poor white trash composing the large majority of the Cotton States."[1] Evidently wearing his mill owner hat, instead of his abolitionist one, Atkinson added, "[For purposes of argument] we may admit that we must have cotton, and that the emancipated slave will be idle and worthless; we may [disregard that] in our southern climate, labor or starvation would be his only choice, and . . . labor upon the cotton field would be the easiest and most profitable way in which he could engage—let him starve and exterminate himself if he will and so remove the Negro question—still we must have cotton."[2]

Throughout the war, Atkinson persistently lobbied for the invasion, occupation, and redistribution of Southern lands for the deliberate purpose of cultivating cotton with free labor. The first opportunity arrived in November 1861, when the federal navy drove off the Confederate defenders at Port Royal Sound, South Carolina. From the Rebel viewpoint, the defeat was sudden and unexpected. Consequently, planters in the area abruptly abandoned their plantations, leaving behind many valuables, including about ten thousand slaves, who had previously composed 80 percent of the population. The region was a center for growing a premium, long-fiber version of cotton termed Sea Island cotton.[3]

On November 8, 1861, federal troops under Brigadier General Thomas Sherman seized the town of Port Royal. Together with the surrounding area known as the Beaufort District, the region produced about fourteen thousand cotton bales annually before the war.[4] The slaves left behind went on a "carnival of idleness" by looting from the homes of their former masters. One federal officer wrote, "The Negroes were perfectly wild, breaking into every building and destroying or carrying off every portable valuable." They destroyed all cotton gins and many tools used in cotton production. Soon, however, Union troops joined them, but they also robbed from the slaves. Blacks attempting to resist were sometimes shot and continually abused by soldiers from the lowest to some of the highest ranks, despite orders from Sherman to the contrary. Former slaves were compelled to labor on government-owned plantations under the eyes of gun-toting federal soldiers. For the former slaves, their long-anticipated freedom proved to be profoundly tested by Union soldiers.[5]

But they were caught between two fires. While some of the evacuating plantation owners advised blacks to remain behind because they would likely starve in the hinterlands, others tried to take their slaves with them. In some instances, slaves failing to obey were shot, and others attempting to hide were accidentally killed as plantation properties were immolated by a combination of evacuating owners, federal soldiers, and freed slaves.[6]

The War Department soon notified Sherman that he must stop the pillage and seize all available cotton. On the recommendation

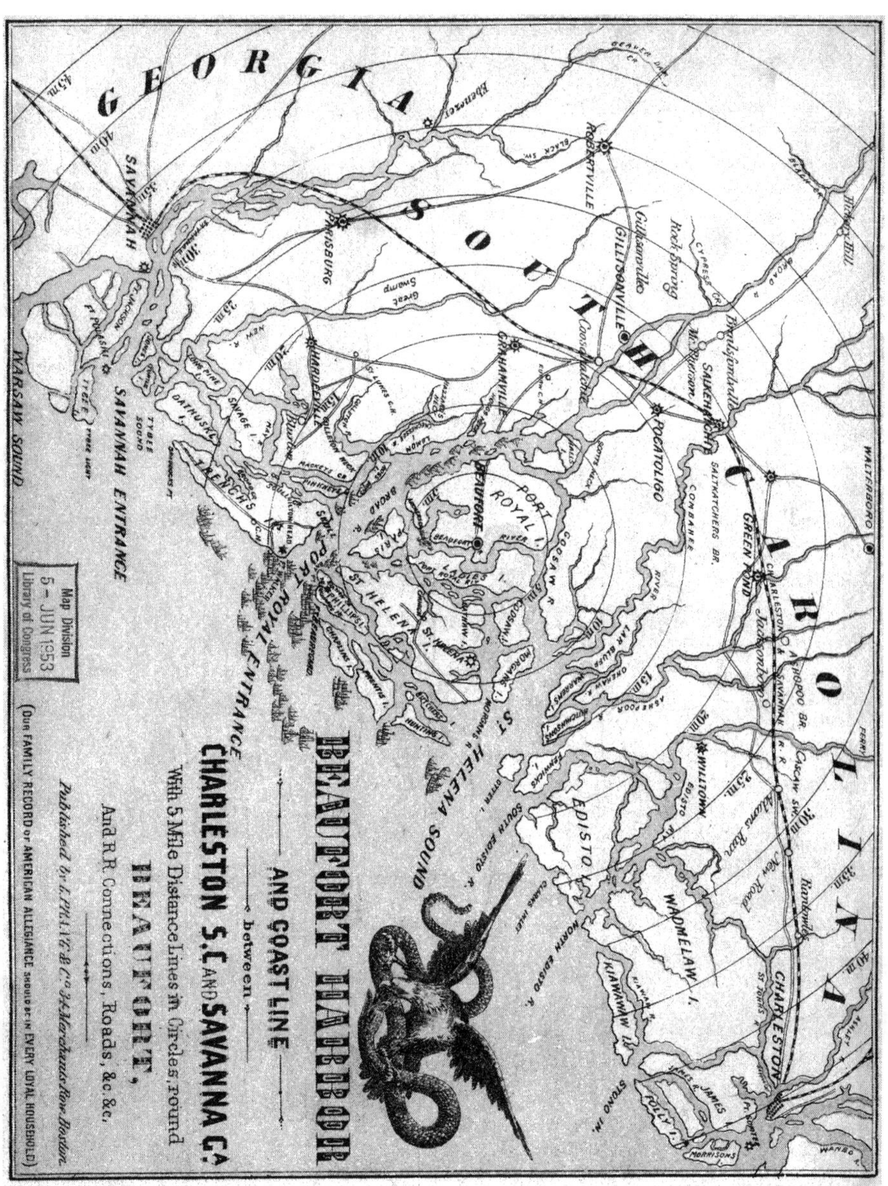


A map of Beaufort Harbor, South Carolina, published in 1861 in Boston. (*Library of Congress*)

of his future son-in-law and the Rhode Island governor, William Sprague, Treasury Secretary Chase assigned Lieutenant Colonel William Reynolds to collect the area's abandoned cotton and sell it at auction in New York. With the aid of former slaves, he was able to harvest a few thousand bales from the 1861 crop, which grossed $500,000 before transportation and other expenses.[7] However, when all expenses were taken into consideration, the venture resulted in a loss of $50,000 to $75,000.[8]

Accordingly, Chase was dissatisfied with Reynolds and abruptly dismissed him after the cotton was delivered. Reynolds and his agents collected fat commissions, and on his departure, an unexplained 10 percent discrepancy remained in his accounts. Nonetheless, after marrying Chase's daughter, Sprague joined with Reynolds and other partners to promote what historian Willie Lee Rose identified as "an illegal private trade in guns and cotton with Confederate agents. It was treason by almost any definition."[9]

Owing to unsettled conditions in the border states, Lincoln was not then prepared to emancipate the Port Royal slaves. Instead, he employed the useful precedent set by General Butler when he was in command at Fortress Monroe, Virginia, and declared escaped slaves to be "contraband of war." They were not free, but neither would they be returned to their Rebel owners. However, Chase was also eager to transform the former slaves into self-sustaining citizens. Consequently, he sent Boston attorney Edward L. Pierce to organize a cotton-growing enterprise to be managed by the federal government but worked by about four thousand contraband blacks. The initiative would also provide education for the former slaves. In March 1862, a group of about fifty men and women, known as Gideonites because of their resemblance to the biblical Gideon's band, arrived to set up schools and preach Christianity.

Pierce and the soon-to-be-dismissed Reynolds fell into persistent squabbling. In one instance, Pierce ordered $6,000 worth of cottonseed from New York without knowing that Reynolds already had an abundant supply. Owing to tardy wage payments, many of the ex-slaves were soon lamenting the loss of "the good times they had when 'old massa' was here." Many spent more time with their pigs

Port Royal Harbor, South Carolina. (*Library of Congress*)

and chickens than in the cotton fields. When Major General David Hunter starting recruiting soldiers among them, many ran away. "Sometimes whole plantations . . . ran into the woods for refuge."[10]

Although Lincoln ordered Hunter to cease recruiting, it took nearly a month for the government-operated plantations to return to normal. Responsibility for Sea Islands plantations was transferred to the War Department in July 1862, and Brigadier General Rufus Saxton took charge of the area. He was made military governor of South Carolina and commander of the Department of the South, both of which mainly comprised the Sea Islands at the time.[11]

Nonetheless, the modest 1861 cotton crop may have partially motivated Congress in June 1862 to augment the direct tax of the August 1861 Revenue Act by enabling it to become a legal pretext for confiscating real estate owned by Southerners in Union-occupied regions of the Confederacy. Owners who did not pay the tax with currency acceptable to collectors—which excluded

Confederate paper—would lose their property for nonpayment of taxes. Terms of sale for lands thus confiscated and later auctioned granted buyers an undisputable title, thereby precluding any chance that the original owners could reclaim them. It was intended that such lands could be used to raise large quantities of cotton under the free-labor system contemplated by Edward Atkinson.

But efforts to grow meaningful quantities of cotton by such methods in the Sea Islands failed, whether on privately owned free-labor plantations or those operated by the federal government. The 1862 crop yielded only twenty-six pounds per acre.[12] The following year, the per-acre yield on government plantations increased but was still only forty-one pounds. While one large, privately owned plantation operated by New Englander Edward Philbrick averaged ninety pounds per acre that year, all yields were far below the antebellum slave-grown average of 135 pounds. The disappointing results chiefly reflected a clash of cultures and poor treatment of the former slaves.[13]

Culturally, the free-labor ethics of New Englanders, typified by the twelve-hour workdays characteristic of textile mills back home, clashed with the lingering customs of former slaves. Ex-slaves considered the unstructured time available after tasks were completed on prewar plantations to be one of their most pleasurable freedoms. One ex-slave announced in a church meeting, "The Yankees preach nothing but cotton, cotton," while the freedman wanted to spend at least some time planting corn and other edibles. In complaint, one Gideonite commented, "The [blacks] are very wayward—now they work and then they stop—and some stop before they begin." Northerners retaliated by evicting, or cutting the rations of, former slaves who failed to work "diligently."[14]

Owing to a chronic food shortage, blacks sought to supplement their diets through hunting and fishing. But Northern superintendents—federal versions of plantation overseers—interpreted such activities as "recreation" and were unwilling to make much time available for them. The Yankees held a similar viewpoint toward the proclivity of ex-slaves to grow foodstuffs. When two workers on one free-labor plantation insisted on the need to plant corn, they were arrested. Essentially, superintendents were forcing ex-slaves to raise cotton in the same manner as before, but without the rations and privileges to which field hands were accustomed on antebellum plantations.[15]

Additionally, former slaves were often paid belatedly, which partly reflected government bureaucracy. One reason the large Philbrick properties were more than twice as productive as those owned by the federal government was that he quickly paid his workers out of his own pocket. His freedmen were paid by the task and did not have to wait until harvest time to be paid. Another reason is that he promised to sell his inexpensively acquired lands to the former slaves after they had saved enough money to buy them, which they erroneously presumed would be at the price *he* had paid. Philbrick also priced each task at a rate based on the performance of the ablest field hand at maximum output in the prewar era. Consequently, few could meet his standard within the allotted time and were required to put in extra time in order to be paid.[16]

By March 1863, confiscations under the direct tax and other authority totaled eighty thousand acres in the Sea Islands. However, only twenty-one thousand were sold to private buyers, and former slaves were able to buy only two thousand of that. White Northern buyers with larger purses frustrated African-American residents who hoped to buy a meaningful share of the auctioned property and thereby become self-sustaining economically.

Philbrick was one of the chief white buyers. Even though he was a prominent abolitionist and former treasurer of the Massachusetts Anti-Slavery Society, he was also a confirmed capitalist who was previously assistant superintendent of the Boston and Worcester Railroad. Through a hastily organized stock company, he purchased one-third of the Sea Island properties available to private buyers in the March 1863 auction at a cost of only one dollar per acre for seven thousand acres.[17] After only a single year, he earned $70,000, or $10 per acre, which translates to a 1,000 percent annual return. Nonetheless, as will be discussed shortly, the returns primarily reflected extraordinary factors, including the bargain price Philbrick paid for the land.[18] As a strong proponent of free enterprise, he reasoned that former slaves would benefit morally, as well as materially, by gaining experience as wage earners under Northern whites.[19]

Owing to the small amounts of land purchased by blacks, Lincoln announced that a second auction of forty thousand acres in fall 1863 would reserve sixteen thousand acres to be sold only in small parcels to persons of African descent. General Saxton felt that it was not enough. Drawing on principles pioneered in the 1862 Homestead Act, he announced regulations that would also give ex-slaves preemptive rights to buy parcels in the twenty-four thousand acres outside the reserve. Much like western homesteaders who, after improving public lands, were permitted to buy their homestead at a fixed price, Saxton proposed similar preferences for the Sea Island blacks.

But Philbrick and others argued that preemptive rights for ex-slaves would rob the US Treasury of a fair price. He also concluded that former slaves were not yet ready to manage their own economic activities. In a letter home, his words reflect an attitude that is almost indistinguishable from the stereotypical Southern planter:

> We find the blacks as dependent as children and as ignorant of social laws as they are of the alphabet. We must stand in relation of parents to them until such time as they can be taught to stand alone, and as in all parental authority, should be tempered by benevolence, sound judgment & firmness, backed if necessary by force.
>
> The fact is that no race of men on God's Earth ever acquired the right to the soil on which they stand without more vigorous exertions than these [former slaves] have made. . . . I cannot see why [they] should be excepted from the general rule.[20]

Most Northerners, including many abolitionists, believed in the merits of a free market. Consequently, in December 1863, Treasury Secretary Chase reversed Saxton's preemptive favoritism for blacks, except for the original sixteen thousand acres of small parcels set aside.[21]

Defeated in their efforts to secure preemptive rights, African-American workers in the Sea Islands sabotaged cotton production on the new Northern-owned plantations, demanded pay raises, petitioned Washington, and denounced Yankee plantation management. Consequently, for the balance of the war, cotton yields remained well below those of the antebellum period. Although the new owners operated profitably, the profits were mostly the result of the inflated cotton prices that prevailed during the war.[22]

As a final blow, ex-slave productivity fell in the second half of 1864, when Northern states were permitted to fill their draft quotas of soldiers by "recruiting" for substitutes among African-Americans in the South. Armed with powers to offer bounties, agents from the North descended on the Sea Islands like a plague of locusts. They randomly seized ex-slaves and often kept the bounties for themselves. One Gideonite wrote that she saw two former slaves shot for attempting to avoid such conscription. A Treasury agent wrote, "The poor Negroes are hunted like wild beasts. . . . There is a perfect panic throughout all these islands. . . . [I can] conceive of no greater terror and distress on the coast of Africa after a slave hunt."[23] During four months of such activities in the Southern states, about twenty-eight hundred African-American soldiers were "recruited" as draft substitutes.[24]

In his study of Northern planters during the Civil War and Reconstruction, Lawrence Powell wrote:

> Those missionaries at Port Royal who wanted the confiscated plantations distributed among freedmen had no stronger argument against the scheme of the tax commissioners [to avoid preemptive rights] than the fact that the "gentlemen who have recently visited Port Royal about land are tempted there alone by present high prices of cotton. Their object seems to be to make the greatest amount of money in the shortest possible time, to run the lands & laborers at the exhaustive point & be off to spend their profits elsewhere." . . . The Yankees who went into cotton planting in these years seem to have regarded the South as . . . a distant colony where men went to make an easy fortune in order to return home and live in comfort.[25]

As cotton prices started tumbling toward the end of the war, Edward Philbrick concluded it would be unprofitable to continue his plantation venture. He was convinced that the ex-slaves would fail to "ever work as they were formerly obliged to and . . . will not produce as much cotton in this generation as they did five years ago." It was an admission that the free-labor cotton production theory espoused by Edward Atkinson did not measure up to his expectations. So Philbrick divided his lands into small parcels, sold them to local workers, and returned to Boston. He permitted African-American buyers to pay half the price of whites, but even at a 50 percent discount, the values were far above the amounts he originally paid. His timing was good. Two years later, in 1867, there were no bidders for government land sales of properties confiscated for nonpayment of taxes.[26]

Despite the disappointing results of the Port Royal Experiment, Edward Atkinson and his followers would later present new proposals for colonizing additional occupied Confederate territories with cheap-cotton-by-free-labor devotees. Meanwhile, however, New England mills and others in need of feedstock would increasingly turn to interbelligerent trade. Within six to eight months after the occupation of Port Royal, new Union military successes in western theaters offered unprecedented opportunities for profit in the cotton market.

*Four*

# Matamoros

THE MEXICAN BORDER WITH TEXAS WAS THE ONLY Confederate boundary immune to the federal blockade. Situated across the Rio Grande from Brownsville, Texas, the port of Matamoros was the single most important legal loophole. Article 7 of the 1848 Treaty of Guadalupe Hidalgo that ended the Mexican-American War specified that the river "should be free and common to the vessels of both countries."[1] Blockading vessels were banned within one mile to the north or south of the river's mouth. Since Matamoros and Brownsville were thirty twisted miles up the shallow river, cargoes were commonly lightered at the beachfront Mexican village of Bagdad.[2]

Despite the advantage provided by a legal circumvention of the blockade, Matamoros trade presented two problems. First, it was distant from the most important parts of the Confederacy. Second, government policies south of the Rio Grande were sometimes conflicting and often corruptly implemented.

It was difficult to ship cargoes to and from Matamoros from most of the Confederacy. The town was hundreds of miles from the nearest important cotton fields in east Texas. The closest rail depot with a line connecting to the Mississippi River was over five hundred miles away. After the first year of the war, Rebel shipments to and from Matamoros were primarily by wagon routes over desert-like terrain that were often short of potable water and nearly devoid of improved roadways. They were never satisfactory for transporting heavy ordnance such as large-caliber artillery.

Early in the war, the most popular course to Brownsville and Matamoros was a waterway along the Texas coast. A long string of sandy islands stretching several hundred miles from Matagorda almost all the way to Mexico provided a shallow passageway between the islands and the mainland. It was navigable to small boats but not the larger vessels of the federal blockading fleet. By early 1862, a steady flow of small vessels glided along the route taking cotton and sugar south and bringing back supplies and contraband, including weapons and munitions. Since the mouth of the Rio Grande was treacherous, most of the boats used Corpus Christi or Baffin Bay as their southernmost port whence cargoes were hauled overland to and from Mexico.[3]

In February 1862, the blockaders retaliated by sending a detachment of marines to Aransas Pass just north of Corpus Christi. Simultaneously, the blockader *Portsmouth* was stationed off the Rio Grande. However, the *Portsmouth* was only temporarily effective in disrupting activities near the mouth of the river because the lighters used to load cargoes onto the deep-water vessels merely shifted their registries to neutral Mexico. Nonetheless, during the ensuing months, a series of unexpected attacks along the Texas coast sufficiently interrupted the trade to drive most of it onshore by July 1862.[4] San Antonio was the concentration point for the overland path. From there it would take six to eight weeks for wagon convoys to reach the Mexican border.[5]

Ultimately, the need for essential goods in the Trans-Mississippi Confederacy combined with the profit incentive motivated traders to tackle the challenging transportation obstacles. At one point, Lieutenant General Edmund Kirby Smith, who commanded the vast region after 1862, said he was getting fifty cents a pound in gold in Mexico for cotton he could buy for four cents a pound in the Rebel interior. Wagon trains of cotton arrived in Matamoros from as far away as Arkansas and Louisiana. One economic historian estimated that about 20 percent of Confederate exports over the span of the war crossed the Mexican border.[6]

The inconsistent governmental policies south of the border reflected a combination of fluctuations in the Mexican central government as well as conflicting power with local authorities along the Rio Grande. Until President Benito Juarez was forced into temporary exile in June 1863, the Mexico City government tended to side with the United States. If Washington could reach an agreement with Mexico to prevent trade across the Rio Grande, the federal blockade could extend along the entire perimeter of the Confederacy. Yet reaching such an agreement was hard for two reasons. One was that states' rights was a respected concept in Mexico just as it was in the Confederacy. The governors of Mexican states along the Texas border favored the trade owing to the tax revenues and economic prosperity it created. Another reason it was hard to reach an agreement was the traditional instability of Mexican governments, temporarily amplified by prospects for European intervention during the Civil War.

## Mexican Politics

Since gaining independence in 1821, Mexico was regularly in political turmoil. There were seventy-five changes in government by the time the American Civil War started in 1861. In January of that year, liberal Benito Juarez assumed the presidency after defeating the armies of the incumbent conservative government. From Mexico City, he held power over the central and southern sections of the country. However, in the states bordering the Rio Grande, local officials assumed more authority. Partly because they could foresee prosperity resulting from trade with the Confederacy, they were wary of interference from Mexico City.[7]

In contrast, Juarez was more concerned with his own political status, which was linked to the welfare of the entire country. He inherited an unmanageable debt totaling $62 million owed to European creditors. By summer 1861, he was compelled to suspend interest payments, which led to a forceful response. In December, Britain, France, and Spain blockaded the port of Veracruz and

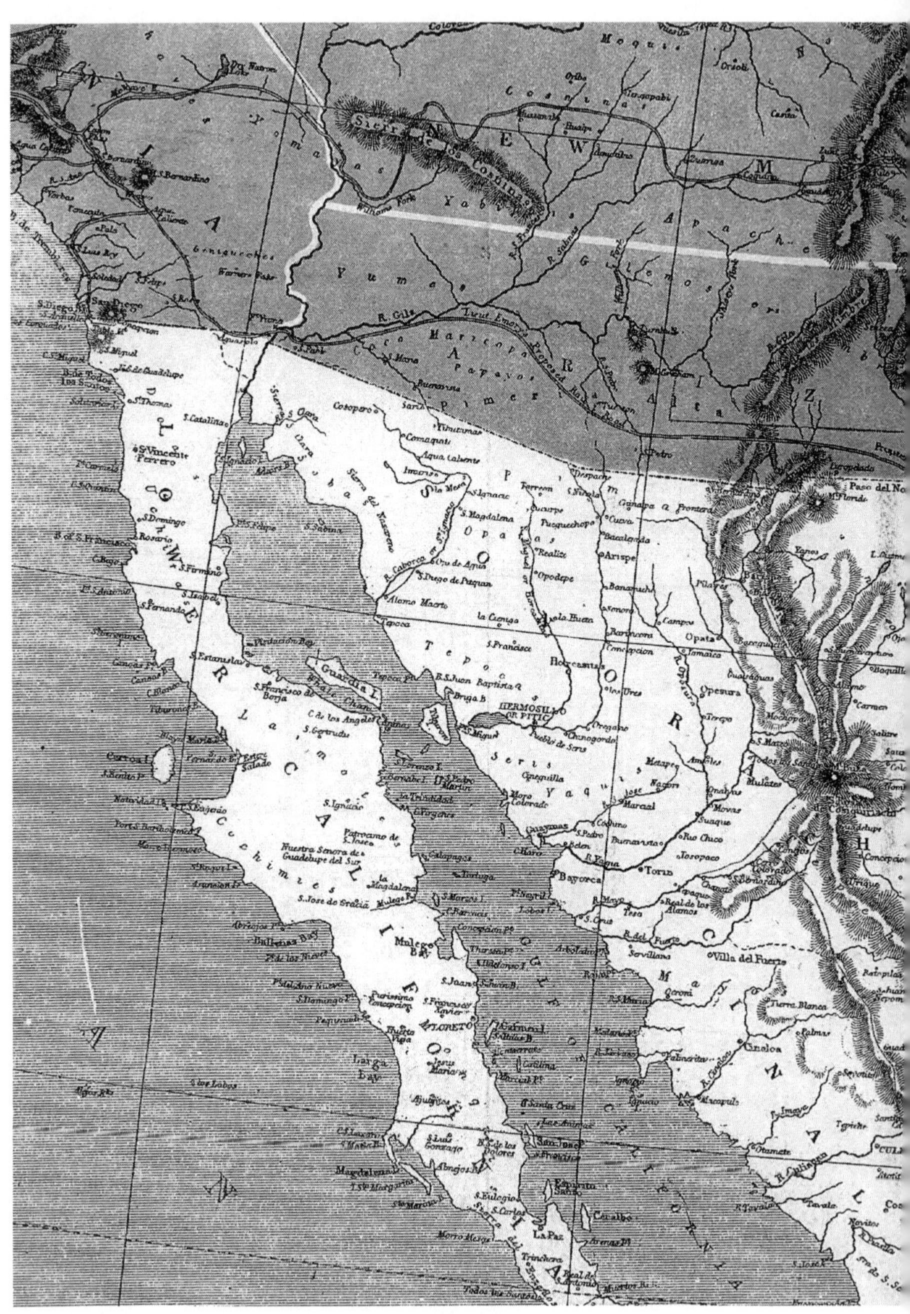


The Mexico and United States border in 1860. (*Library of Congress*)

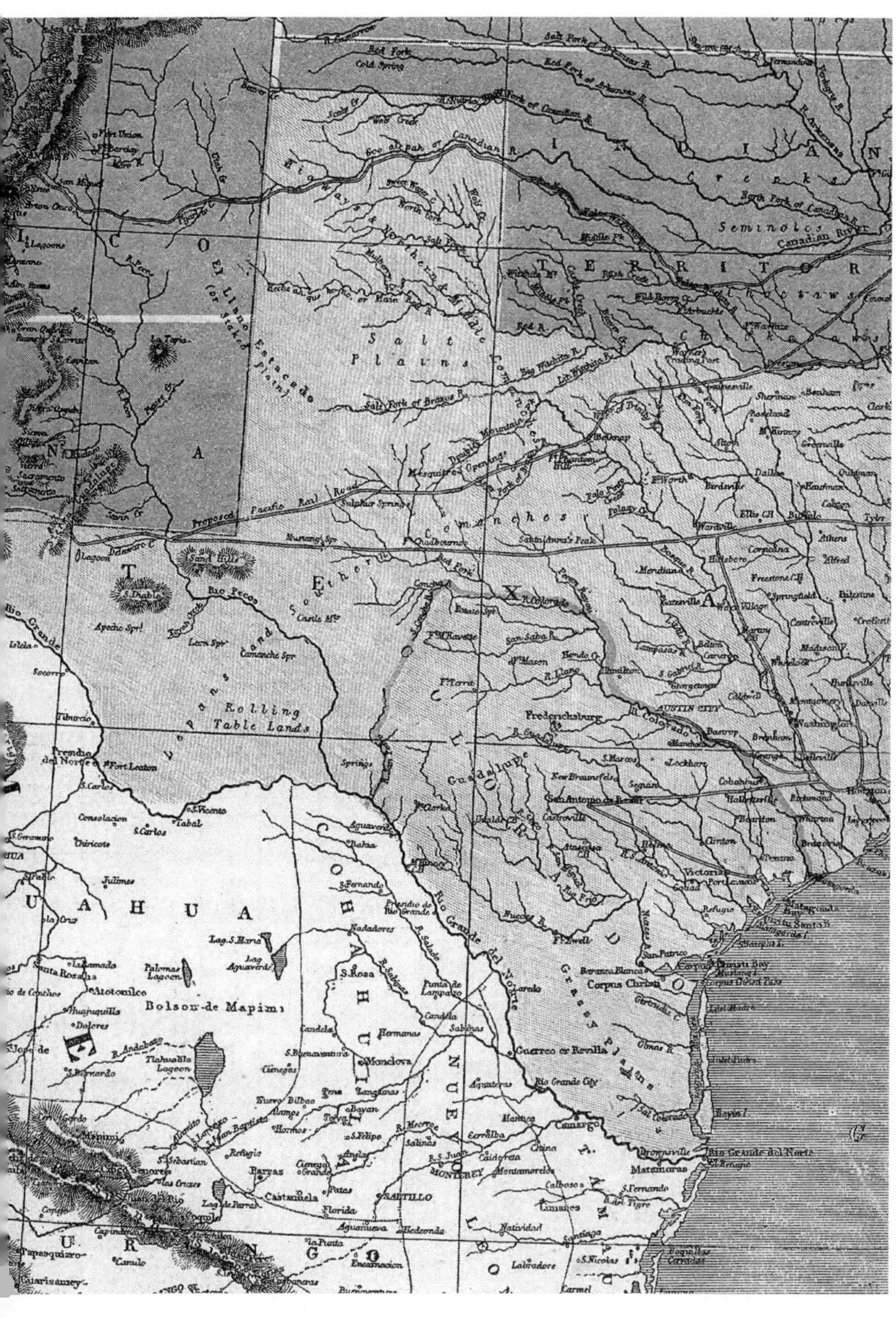
Salt Plains
Seminoles
Creeks
El Llano Estacado (or Staked Plains)
Proposed Pacific Rail Road
Camanches
Rolling Table Lands
Sand Hills
S. Diablo
Rio Pecos
Rio Grande
R. Colorado
AUSTIN CITY
Fredericksburg
San Antonio de Bexar
New Braunfels
Lockhart
Bastrop
Washington
Victoria
Goliad
Refugio
Corpus Christi
Corpus Christi Bay
Grassy Plains
Laredo
Guerrero or Revilla
Rio Grande City
Camargo
Brownsville
Matamoras
Rio Grande del Norte
MONTEREY
SALTILLO
Monclova
Bolson de Mapimi
Palomas Lagoon
Santa Rosalia
Presidio de Rio Grande
Presidio del Norte
Fort Leaton
S. Fernando
Santiago
Linares
Labradore
Salt Fork of Brazos R.
Big Wachita R.
Canadian R.
Red Fork of Arkansas R.
Sherman
Dallas
Waco Village
Belton
Gonzales
Seguin
Castroville
Dist. Bahia
Corpus Christi Pass
Padre I.
Mustang I.
Matagorda
San Patricio
Nueces R.
Nadadores
Candela
Sabinas
Hermanos
Parras
Castañuela
Patos
Florida
Aguanueva
Hedeonda

seized the customs houses, where they collected tariffs and applied the funds toward reducing Mexico's debt. By March 1862, a French army arrived, which prompted a withdrawal by the British and Spanish, who concluded that France was attempting to establish a vassal government instead of merely solving an international monetary disagreement. On May 5, 1862 (Cinco de Mayo), when the French army attempted to advance toward Mexico City, it was defeated by Mexicans. Nonetheless, the French returned a year later to win a victory and capture Mexico City in June 1863. Juarez was forced to exile his government to the northern state of Chihuahua, which borders El Paso.

By October 1863, a member of Austria's royal family, Ferdinand Maximilian, tentatively accepted an invitation from Mexican conservatives to become emperor of Mexico.[8] Partially influenced by his Spanish-born wife, Empress Eugenie de Montijo, Napoleon III was the mastermind behind the maneuver. He intended that the Hapsburg family member become a puppet monarch. Maximilian assumed the throne in April 1864, but would not be secure until armed resistance from Juarez was subdued. But defeating Juarez was unlikely without the presence of an occupying French army.[9]

Prior to being ousted from Mexico City, Juarez attempted to negotiate an alliance with the United States that would temporarily satisfy European creditors. He hoped it would delay French intervention long enough for him to stabilize the government and craft a more lasting debt solution. He and Lincoln's representative, Thomas Corwin, hammered out a proposal for the United States to lend $11 million to Mexico, secured by a mortgage on public lands in northern Mexican states such as Baja California. Since the Confederates employed an inept diplomat in Mexico City and could not hope to offer comparable financial terms, Juarez pinned his hopes for placating the Europeans on the United States. But the Juarez-Corwin agreement never became effective due to disinterest in Congress together with procrastinating and insincere advocacy in Lincoln's administration.[10]

Meanwhile, diplomatic arrangements in the states bordering the Rio Grande proceeded independently. The head negotiators were a

Mexican governor named Santiago Vidaurri and a Confederate commissioner named Jose Quintero. Initially, Vidaurri controlled the two states immediately upstream from Tamaulipas, which is the state where Matamoros and the mouth of the Rio Grande are located. However, he was not without influence in Tamaulipas, and by spring 1862 he had control of it.[11] Vidaurri worried that Juarez would challenge his authority and went so far as to propose annexation of his territory by the Confederacy as a means of securing protection against Juarez. President Davis declined the annexation offer but welcomed an eagerness to trade.[12]

Partly because of historical political turmoil, Vidaurri had difficulty maintaining control of his region to the end of the war. Various bandits who raided on both sides of the border sporadically challenged his authority. Most notable was a polished and likable scoundrel named Carvajal, who befriended the Confederates. For a time, Carvajal set up a recruiting station in Brownsville under the protection of Rebel Colonel John S. "Rip" Ford. Vidaurri responded by raising the tax on cotton imported into Mexico, which prompted Ford's superior to order the arrest of Carvajal.

Finally, when Juarez relocated to nearby Chihuahua in summer 1863, Vidaurri felt compelled to seek safety with the French army, thereby leaving Juarez in charge of the Rio Grande trade by default. Although his earlier favoritism toward the United States suggested he might shut down the trade, it was simply too profitable and remained wide open until the end of the war. Two years after it ended, Juarez defeated Maximilian's forces, executed the Hapsburg monarch, and regained control of the government in Mexico City. After leaving the border, Vidaurri joined Maximilian; he was likewise executed in 1867. Juarez remained president of Mexico until his death by heart attack in 1871.[13]

## Trade Characteristics

Despite difficult routes to the Confederate hinterland, trade through Matamoros began before the end of 1861, for two reasons. First was the reduced risk of cargo loss that resulted from the Mexican port's legal immunity to the Union blockade. Second, despite an unofficial cotton embargo during the first year of the war, the Confederate Congress specifically exempted exports across the Rio Grande. The exemption enabled Trans-Mississippi growers to profit from crops they were otherwise expected to destroy. Given a choice between burning their inventory and selling it, many planters were sufficiently motivated to accept the arduous journey to the Mexican market.

An estimated five thousand wagons were used to haul cotton from Texas, Louisiana, Arkansas, and the Indian Territory (present-day Oklahoma). San Antonio and Alleyton, near Houston, were collection points, which remained hundreds of arid miles distant from depots on the Texas side of the Rio Grande. Even in good weather it would take four to six weeks to finish the trip. Wagon trains typically consisted of ten to fifteen vehicles, each carrying about twenty cotton bales. The trains were in constant danger of attack by bushwhackers, Native Americans, bandits, and outlaws. As noted, a smaller amount moved to the Rio Grande on coastal vessels. The ships were nearly all sail driven, carried forty to eighty bales each, and drew only about three feet of water. Despite such restrictive conveyances, it is estimated that over three hundred thousand bales were moved through Matamoros during the war.[14]

Over the next three-and-a-half years, twenty thousand speculators flocked to Matamoros. English became so commonly spoken that the *Matamoros Morning Call* newspaper was published in the language. A regularly scheduled packet line was set up to Havana, Cuba, carrying a great deal of arms and ammunition for the Confederacy. By 1863, regular steamship service to London was established. The following year, federally occupied New Orleans offered two regularly scheduled steamships. Matamoros effectively became a blockade-free Confederate port. At one point in summer 1864, twenty-four ships in the New Orleans harbor were destined for Matamoros. Furthermore, one of the city's newspapers advertised more departures for the Mexican port than any other destination.[15]

While most Matamoros trade was presumably with Europe, merchants from Northern states also participated. Prior to the war,

"Loading wagons on the Calle de Cesar, Matamoras, for Piedras Negras [1864]." (*Library of Congress*)

scarcely one ship annually left New York for Matamoros, but from summer 1861 to summer 1864, the average was about one per week—a fiftyfold increase. Confederate Brigadier General Hamilton Bee said that arms could be bought in New York and shipped to Matamoros and thence imported into Texas. The *New York Herald* wrote about a Gotham shipper principally engaged in contraband trade via the Mexican town. By the last year of the war, trade between New York and Matamoros averaged a million dollars a week.[16]

In their book *Napoleon III and Mexico,* authors Alfred Hanna and Kathryn Hanna wrote, "Officers of blockading vessels were incensed by the purchase of Confederate cotton by Northerners; they were outraged particularly by the number of ships from New York and other Eastern ports engaged illicitly in this traffic."[17]

According to historian Robert Kerby, Matamoros trade from Northern and Union-occupied Southern ports was a significant source of war supplies for Rebel armies west of the Mississippi River. "Profits earned from the sale of cotton were either collected in gold or reinvested in manufactures, provisions, or munitions-of-war carried to Bagdad by inbound ships. Most of the vessels . . . and imports . . . were . . . European, but it was not uncommon for ships flying the flag of the United States to bring down cargoes of contraband from Boston, New York, or Philadelphia."[18]

Cargoes from Northern states included large quantities of munitions and war supplies for the Confederate army. There were also a sizable number of wagons and harnesses, as well as thousands of pistols, carbines, uniforms, shoes, blankets, and other materials manufactured in Northern states. Civilian goods also arrived from the North. One San Antonio newspaper reported that the very paper it was printed on came from New York and that cotton traders returning from Matamoros sometimes carried gold marked by the Philadelphia mint.

Shippers between New York and Matamoros used direct and broken-voyage methods to transport goods. The direct method utilized bogus front men in Mexico and ordinary brokers in New York. However, if direct clearance between the two ports could not be secured, the broken-voyage system was used to circumvent interdiction. Shipments destined for either Matamoros or New York would first stop at such neutral ports as Havana, Nassau, or even Halifax with legitimate papers for the first leg of the journey. Once at the intermediate point, authorization for the second half of the journey would be obtained.

Ironically, the British became particularly annoyed at trade between Matamoros and ports in the Northern states or Union-occupied ones in the South. The British Foreign Office received a steady stream of complaints from shippers in their country about the advantages of US shippers in the Matamoros market. Specifically, they complained that federal blockaders would stop British-flagged vessels for inspection and confiscation of contraband items while ships trading between New York and the Rio Grande passed unmolested. Consequently, British foreign secretary Lord Russell warned Secretary of State Seward that "hostilities" against British vessels bound for Matamoros could lead to a "calamity" between the two nations.[19]

Charles Stillman is a prominent example of a Matamoros trader with family ties to the Northern states. Born in Connecticut, he was fifty when the war broke out and had been in Texas and Mexico for over thirty years. He had disputed ownership of large land tracks north of the Rio Grande near Brownsville. He also founded

Brownsville in 1849, naming it after nearby Fort Brown. Although he married a New England lady, she could not abide the region's climate and relocated to New York with their children in 1853. Charles visited the family during the summers but otherwise stayed in Texas and Mexico. He claimed that he grew to dislike "Yankees," whom he regarded as "haughty and domineering." By 1861, he declared, "My sympathy is for the South. In fact I never wish to see the North again."[20]

However, Stillman camouflaged his Southern sympathies by using three Mexicans in Matamoros and Monterrey to handle his mail and contracts. Much of his cotton was obtained from a Confederate Texan who switched sides in November 1863 when Brownsville was temporarily occupied by Union troops. The converted Union-loyal man set up a new partnership that included Stillman, which ran a constantly moving chain of at least three ships between Matamoros and New York. The partnership benefitted from blockade policies designed to supply cotton to Northern providers of military uniforms. Consequently, Stillman sold Texas cotton to the federal government for use in making uniforms for federal soldiers.[21]

Stillman's Matamoros-bound cargoes normally originated at New York. To minimize customs interference, his partnership registered its three ships under the British flag. When preparing to leave New York, the ships would generally seek clearance directly to Matamoros, but if necessary they would settle for authorization to travel to a neutral port such as Havana before continuing on to Matamoros. Stillman's ships typically carried cotton to New York and returned munitions and other contraband evidently obtained from suppliers in the Northern states. By 1864, a congressional committee began investigating Stillman's business, but it discovered that his New York agent, James Donahue, had disappeared and could not testify, while Stillman remained beyond reach in Mexico.[22]

Early in 1865, Stillman suffered a stroke. Because the war was winding down and trade volumes along with it, he decided to rejoin his family in a more comfortable New York setting. But the congressional investigation left him with a desire to avoid attracting attention, and he sought to reenter the United States quietly. He first traveled to Great Britain before boarding a New York-bound steamer as a supercargo in order to avoid having his name appear on the passenger list. (A supercargo is an individual who travels with a shipper's cargo and assumes responsibility for managing and delivering it. He is essentially a caretaker, much like an apartment superintendent.) A few months after arriving in New York, Stillman received a pardon from President Andrew Johnson.[23]

After the war, Stillman was one of the richest men in the United States. Among other investments, he became a prominent shareholder of New York's National City Bank, which was the predecessor to today's Citicorp. His son, grandson, and great-grandson each became the bank's board chairman, with the great-grandson holding the position as late as 1967. Two granddaughters married into the Rockefeller family. Stillman died in 1875, about ten years after moving to New York.[24]

William Sprague is an even more prominent example of a distinguished Union leader ensnared in dubious Matamoros commerce. In the first days of the war in April 1861, the thirty-one-year-old Sprague, then governor of Rhode Island, organized a state regiment that was one of the first to reach Washington as President Lincoln waited anxiously for protectors to arrive in the event of a Rebel attempt to capture the city. He also participated at the First Battle of Bull Run. Only five years earlier, he had inherited his father's prosperous business that was founded on cotton textiles but included locomotive manufacturing, among other interests. By the end of 1862, he was anxiously seeking raw cotton for his mills.

Sprague, who became one of Rhode Island's US senators in March 1863, formed a partnership with Harris Hoyt, a putative Union-loyal Texan. Hoyt approached Treasury Secretary Chase for the necessary cotton-trading permits but was denied them. Sprague soon became involved with Chase because of the romantic interest he developed for the secretary's twenty-two-year-old daughter, Kate. The two were married in November 1863. At the wedding, Kate wore a $50,000 tiara gift from her husband. Afterward she promptly began decorating their sixty-room Rhode Island mansion and using the senator's influence and wealth to promote her father's presidential ambitions.

Senator William Sprague of the state of Rhode Island. (*Library of Congress*)

Although it was unable to get cotton-trading permits, Hoyt, Sprague & Company purchased three vessels. (Ironically, one of them, the *Ella Warley,* would accidentally collide with *The Star of the West,* the ship that President James Buchanan had employed in a failed effort to provide relief to Fort Sumter before the war began during the secession crisis. Both ships sank about ten miles from New York.) Hoyt quickly sailed one of the ships to Havana, where he changed its name and adopted a British registry. The vessel next sailed to Matamoros with a cargo of guns, rifles, cartridges, caps, gunpowder, and other contraband. The goods were finally shipped to Houston, where Hoyt reached an agreement with the Confederate government to supply $400,000 of similar merchandise in exchange for cotton.[25]

About two years later, in November 1864, the Union army arrested Charles Prescott, who skippered Hoyt's ship. On December 6, 1864, Prescott provided a full confession, which led to the arrest of two Hoyt, Sprague & Company partners, including one of the senator's first cousins. Panicked that he would be charged with treason, the senator wrote unconvincing denials to Major General John Dix, who had ultimate authority of the investigation. As the enquiry expanded, Hoyt also implicated Senator Sprague, who was eventually arraigned on six charges of treason. Fortunately for Sprague, Dix himself had compiled a questionable record of interbelligerent trade when commanding occupation troops in Norfolk, Virginia. Dix pardoned the three Hoyt, Sprague partners who confessed and left the matter of the senator's prosecution up to Secretary of War Stanton.[26]

In correspondence, Sprague referred to the incident as Hoyt's "Texas Adventure." Messages the senator wrote at the time of the "Texas Adventure" to General Butler in New Orleans and the "Officer Commanding the Gulf Squadron, Gulf of Mexico" reveal that he almost certainly was aware of the mission. But the assassination of President Lincoln in April 1865 soon shifted public attention. Officially, Stanton took no further action, but the compiled evidence was accessible should he and Sprague ever battle politically.

After the war, its very existence may have been an unspoken threat during the Senate vote in 1868 on whether to convict Lincoln's successor, President Andrew Johnson, on the articles of impeachment brought against him by the House. Sprague's father-in-law presided over the proceedings as chief justice and probably opposed impeachment because he believed the contested Tenure of Office Act was unconstitutional. Essentially, the act denied President Johnson the authority to replace selected civil officeholders whenever the Senate was not in session, which was comparatively frequent during the era. The secretary of war was one such officeholder. When Johnson tried to replace Stanton, who was resisting the president's Reconstruction policies, the impeachment charges were drawn up against the president. The trial took place in the Senate, where Stanton obviously desired Johnson's conviction. Sprague voted for conviction, which Johnson avoided by a single vote.[27]

Thereafter, the cracks in William and Kate's marriage grew into publicly visible fractures, leading it to collapse. Both fled to extramarital affairs, with Kate choosing New York senator Roscoe Conkling, whom William once ran off with a shotgun. Conkling was one of the most flamboyant figures to walk on America's political stage. At six-foot-three, "Lord Roscoe" dressed outlandishly, with ornate vests and white flannel trousers, thereby giving "the appearance of strutting even while sitting down."[28] Kate often traveled to Europe, spending huge amounts of her husband's money. William became an alcoholic. The family fortune took a serious blow in the Panic of 1873, and the couple divorced nine years later.

Ever since assuming command from General Butler in New

Orleans in December 1862, Union Major General Nathaniel Banks was anxious to move against Texas. A former speaker of the House, Banks had been a congressman from Massachusetts. He worked as a bobbin boy in the state's textile industry as a youth. Consequently, he was sensitive to the demands from his home state for access to cheap cotton. Less than two months before Banks arrived in New Orleans, Secretary Stanton sent notes to the governors of New York and the New England states saying that Banks was organizing an army for the purpose of occupying parts of Texas. He urged the governors to provide army volunteers and implied that the ensuing military invasion would provide Texas lands for white Northerners to cultivate cotton, much like had been attempted in Port Royal. On October 30, 1862, the *New York Times* editorialized, "Texas needs to be colonized as well as captured. New England and the Middle states must furnish the new population for Texas."[29]

Nonetheless, the November 1862 national elections provoked a shift in military plans. Republican losses in states northwest of the Ohio River convinced Lincoln that clearing the Mississippi River for unobstructed commerce was more important. A warning from Indiana's governor, Oliver P. Morton, particularly influenced Lincoln's decision:

> The fate of the North-West is trembling in the balance. The results of the late [autumn 1862] election admonishes all who understand its import that not an hour is to be lost. . . . During the recent campaign, it was the staple of every democratic speech, that we of the North-West had no interests or sympathies in common with the people of the Northern and Eastern States; that New England is fattening at our expense; that the people of New England are cold, selfish, money-making and through the medium of tariffs and railroads are pressing us to dust; . . . that socially and commercially [our] sympathies are with those of the people of the Southern States rather than with the people of the North and East; that the Mississippi river is the great artery and outlet of all Western commerce; that the people

> of the North-West can never consent to be separated politically from the people who control the mouth of that river. . . . And I give it here as my deliberate judgment, that should the misfortune of arms, or other cause, compel us to the abandonment of this War and the concession of the independence of the Rebel States, that Ohio, Indiana, and Illinois can only be prevented . . . from a new act of secession . . . by a bloody and desolating Civil War.[30]

Therefore, by December, Banks was told that he must first aid Major General Ulysses Grant in freeing the Mississippi River from Rebel fortifications. Accordingly, while Grant held Vicksburg in a death grip, Banks laid siege to the companion Rebel fortress at Port Hudson, Louisiana, which fell shortly after Vicksburg in July 1863. Not until November 1863 was he able to send an expeditionary force to capture Brownsville. In response, the Rebels burned the town's available cotton and, like the trail of an ant colony raiding a jar of honey, shifted their Rio Grande caravans to fordable points two hundred to three hundred miles upstream such as Eagle Pass and Laredo. Until the Confederates recaptured Brownsville nine months later, upstream Mexican towns such as Piedras Negras became prosperous cotton trading centers and duty collection points. The change also enriched the Texas families of King and Kenedy, who had a monopoly on Rio Grande steamboat traffic. Their pilots were the masters of the river's tortuous channels and unpredictable currents. The Kings later became more famous cattle barons as owners of the King Ranch. At Matamoros, the result was a moderate decline in traffic and sharp increase in transportation costs due to the lengthy detours.[31]

Federal soldiers were able to hold Brownsville for only nine months. Confederates recaptured the town in July 1864. Thereafter, trade volume through the upriver villages declined to insignificance. The shorter routes through Brownsville led to a resurgence of commerce. In August 1864, a visitor to Matamoros wrote, "There are millions of dollars of merchandise in the place. Every room . . . capable of holding a man was rented at a large price." Simultaneously, the US consul in Matamoros complained that "large quantities of merchandise now cross the river daily . . . [the Rebels] having taken advantage of the absence of our troops." During October and November alone, three hundred tons of ordnance passed through Brownsville and on to San Antonio. By Christmas, San Antonio was experiencing such a boom that specie was once again the common currency in the city's markets, whereas hard money had nearly vanished everywhere else in the Confederacy.[32]

Eventually one federal naval commander decided to test the international legitimacy of open trade at Matamoros. On February 25, 1863, Acting Rear Admiral Charles Wilkes instructed the USS *Vanderbilt* to stop and board the British-flagged merchant ship *Peterhoff* as the latter was leaving the neutral port of St. Thomas in the Danish West Indies. Although the boarding party learned the *Peterhoff* was officially bound for Matamoros, it also discovered evidence that most of the cargo was contraband destined for the Confederates in Texas. As a result, the ship was seized and taken to a New York prize court. The chief matter for adjudication was whether a neutral-flagged merchant ship could be seized when bound from one neutral port to another. Admiral Wilkes stirred up considerable animosity, which resulted in British saber rattling across the Atlantic.

While the matter was under litigation, Lincoln unilaterally took steps to relax international tensions and restrict the flexibility of Union naval commanders to initiate similar provocations against powerful European neutrals. First, he directed that the *Peterhoff*'s mail pouch be delivered unopened to British authorities. Second, he instructed Navy Secretary Gideon Welles to advise all ship commanders that they "will avoid the reality, and as far as possible, the appearance of using any neutral port to watch neutral vessels and then dart out to seize them on their departure. . . . Complaint has been made that this has been the practice at the port of St. Thomas which practice, if it exists, is disapproved, and must cease."[33]

Although the *Peterhoff*'s seizure appeared to be illegal, the prize court condemned the ship, which was purchased by the federal government, armed, and added to a blockading squadron. Ironically, less than a year later, the renamed USS *Peterhoff* was mistakenly sunk by another federal warship when it was incorrectly assumed to be a blockade-runner. Two years after the Civil War, the Supreme Court overruled the decision of New York's wartime prize court and concluded that Wilkes's seizure was unlawful. The author of the court's opinion was Chief Justice Salmon P. Chase.[34]

After the fall of Vicksburg, the Confederate Trans-Mississippi depended almost entirely on cotton trade to obtain the necessities of war and many of the things required to merely avoid hunger and provide shelter for civilians. There were essentially two markets for the cotton. One was export, either across the Rio Grande or via blockade-runners. The other was overland trade directly with enemy agents infiltrating through enemy lines. Although Matamoros would remain important after the fall of Vicksburg, Trans-Mississippi Confederates would increasingly rely on growing interbelligerent trading at Shreveport, Louisiana, and along tributaries of the Mississippi River.

*Five*

# Mississippi Valley Trade

A COUPLE OF MONTHS AFTER THE WAR BEGAN, TREASURY Secretary Chase adopted a "follow the flag" trade policy. Specifically, he intended that cotton traders be allowed to accompany Union armies as Rebel territories were occupied. In the western theater, the initial motivation was to sell provender from the Ohio and upper Mississippi River valleys. The breakdown in prewar supply lines inflated prices below the Ohio River, where corn was priced at forty to fifty cents a bushel, compared to twenty cents on the right bank.[1] However, as indicated by the map on page 61, when Brigadier General Ormsby Mitchel took his division of Major General Don Carlos Buell's Army of the Ohio into south-central Tennessee and north Alabama in April 1862, they were among the first federals to enter rich cotton fields. Traders quickly learned there were greater profits in buying cotton for the North than in selling provender to Southerners.

Estimating that at least ten thousand cotton bales were available in the area, Mitchel invited New York buyers into the region, including his son-in-law, W. B. Hook. Unfortunately for the general, some of his letters to Hook including one advising the younger man that "it is the bold man who wins" were captured by the

Confederates. A Rebel general forwarded the correspondence to Union General Buell, presumably to reveal Mitchel's self-serving commercial activities. Senator Zachariah Chandler of Michigan later accused the army of stealing $2 million of north Alabama cotton. William Sprague charged that army officers bought all the cotton they could while seizing all that Northern businessmen purchased, presumably including Sprague's representatives.[2]

By July 1862, Union armies captured and thereafter continuously occupied three cotton-trading centers on the Mississippi River: New Orleans, Memphis, and Helena, Arkansas. Major General Samuel Curtis, who was the victor at the March 1862 battle of Pea Ridge, Arkansas, fortified Helena. After the battle of Shiloh, Major General William T. Sherman was in charge at Memphis. General Butler held New Orleans after it fell to Admiral David Farragut. The Mississippi Delta of that region provided some of the world's richest cotton-growing land. Simultaneously, about three-fourths of New England's textile spindles were idled owing to a shortage of feedstock. Historian David Surdam wrote, "During the Civil War many cotton planters along the Mississippi River chose self-interest over nationalism. Trade resumed at New Orleans and Memphis, as well as many smaller towns. More than 600,000 bales of cotton were exported from Memphis and New Orleans."[3]

## Memphis

Two weeks before Memphis was occupied in June 1862, eighteen textile manufacturers petitioned Massachusetts congressman Samuel Cooper to reestablish trade there. Merchants in Cincinnati, St. Louis, and Louisville feverishly anticipated opening commerce at Memphis.[4] As Memphis trade began during summer 1862, a Treasury agent tried to restrict it to a select group of individuals, but the result was that smuggling soon began in earnest.[5] When Major General Henry Halleck took over Grant's army after the April 1862 battle of Shiloh in western Tennessee, he encouraged more official trade, partly out of sympathy for the suffering population. As Confederate armies withdrew, they often impressed food supplies and livestock from area residents.

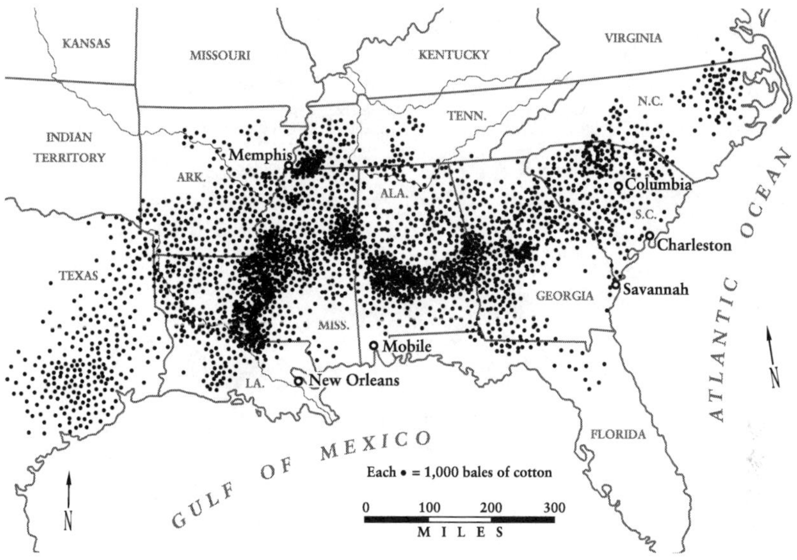


Cotton Production in the South, 1860.

In his personal memoirs, General Grant explained his reaction to Washington's decision authorizing interbelligerent commerce:

> [T]he government wanted to get out all the cotton possible from the South. . . . Pay in gold was authorized, and stations on the Mississippi River and on the railroad . . . had to be designated where cotton would be received. This opened to the enemy not only the means of converting cotton into money . . . but it afforded them means of obtaining accurate and intelligent information in regard to our position and strength. It was also demoralizing to the troops. Citizens obtaining permits from the treasury department had to be protected . . . to get out cotton by which they realized enormous profits. Men who had enlisted to fight . . . did not like to be engaged in protecting a traffic which went to the support of an enemy . . . and the profits of which went to men who shared none of their dangers.[6]

By July, a correspondent for the *St. Louis Republican* reported that Memphis railroads groaned with cotton transported north.[7] When Grant and Sherman attempted to outlaw the use of gold in cotton transactions, they did not realize the potent influence of international politics. Each must have been puzzled that Secretary of War Stanton ordered them (through Halleck, who had been promoted to general in chief and relocated to Washington) to back down, because he normally opposed interbelligerent trade. However, he was pressured by Secretary of State Seward, who was sensitive to the feedstock needs of the British textile industry, which could foresee empty warehouses within a few months. Essentially, the British concluded that if gold transactions were permitted, more cotton would reach the market. In his order to once again permit gold-for-cotton purchases in the Memphis region, Halleck explained that the practice would be consistent with the habit of General Butler in New Orleans.[8]

Lincoln ordered Halleck "to see that all possible facilities are afforded for getting out cotton. It is deemed important to get as much as we can to market."[9] Revealing an anti-Semitic side to his personality, Sherman complained that Halleck's order "is worse than a defeat. The country will swarm with dishonest Jews who will smuggle powder, pistols, and percussion caps . . . in spite of all the guards we can provide."[10] In his PhD dissertation, Robert Futrell wrote that "considerable amounts of gold were going south at this time, carried in cleverly designed money belts by unscrupulous traders. . . . [The] Adams Express Company in Cairo . . . [listed] $355,000 in gold receipts from September 9th to November 30th. [There] is little reason to doubt that all of this coin was secretly carried into Tennessee, Arkansas, and Mississippi [for] cotton."[11]

Effects of the Memphis cotton trade were soon evident in the strengthening Confederate armed resistance. By October 1862, Major General Earl Van Dorn's Rebel army was ready to challenge Grant. Because Grant was temporarily in St. Louis, Van Dorn's attack hit Union Major General William Rosecrans at Corinth. Although Rosecrans was able to hold the fortified town, Van Dorn would have been unable to assume the initiative but for supplies received through Memphis.[12] One detective wrote Grant that railroad employees were involved in a smuggling ring that furnished Confederates with many revolvers and carbines.[13] Sherman complained that Cincinnati provided more supplies to the Confederacy than Charleston, South Carolina, which was one of the chief entrepots for blockade-runners.[14]

On December 17, 1862, as he prepared to launch what would turn out to be an unsuccessful maneuver to attack Vicksburg by an overland route from west Tennessee, Grant issued General Order Number 11, banning Jewish traders from his military district. "The Jews as a class, violating every regulation of trade established by the Treasury Department and also Department Orders, are hereby expelled from the Department." Earlier he had written, "The Jews seem to be a privileged class that can travel anywhere. They will land at any wood yard or landing on the river and make their way through the country." The order and remarks were particularly offensive to the many Jewish traders in Memphis and Cincinnati. Within three weeks, General in Chief Halleck telegraphed from Washington, instructing Grant to revoke the order.[15]

The following month, War Secretary Stanton sent a trusted assistant, Charles Dana, to investigate cotton trade at Memphis. Dana wrote back:

> The mania for sudden fortunes made in cotton raging in the vast population . . . of this town almost [exceeds] the numbers . . . of residents . . . and has demoralized the army. Every colonel, captain, or quartermaster is in secret partnership with some operator of cotton. . . . I had no conception of the extent of the evil until I came and saw for myself.[16]

Historian Ludwell Johnson wrote that later in the war, an authorized Memphis agent named Ellery explained "how his room was besieged from seven o'clock every morning by mobs of people begging for contracts, mobs that included many 'persuasive' women whose blandishments Ellery did not find at all disagreeable."[17] Similarly, historian Merton Coulter wrote:

"Memphis was the center of truly gigantic traffic directly with the Confederacy. A Federal army officer charged that, 'Memphis has been of more value to the Southern Confederacy since it fell than [the neutral blockade-running concentration port of] Nassau.' . . . [Michigan] Senator Chandler charged that through July 1864 an estimated $20-$30 million of supplies had gone to the Confederacy through Memphis alone."[18]

In spring 1864, a Mississippi resident wrote Confederate secretary of war James Seddon to complain of a demoralizing breakdown in respect for private property. It seemed like nearly everyone was stealing cotton stored in remote locations and selling it to Northern traders. Even the normally most respectable and unlikely citizens were involved:

"Ladies residing in this region, eminent for wealth, respectability, intelligence, and beauty, make nothing of taking government cotton without authority and traveling in the night to the enemy's lines . . . bribing both [Rebel and Union] pickets, and in return bringing out whisky, calico, and coffee, and [selling] it . . . at a large profit."[19]

After Sherman assumed a field command in November 1862, the new Memphis commander became Major General Stephen Hurlbut, who was a Lincoln friend from Illinois. While Hurlbut was in charge at Memphis, the widow of President James K. Polk wrote Richmond from Nashville in January 1864, asking permission to send her cotton to Memphis, where it could be sold. In April 1864, Major General Cadwallader Washburn replaced Hurlbut. Washburn was known to oppose interbelligerent trade. The following month he wrote Secretary of War Stanton that 95 percent of the trade at Memphis went to disloyal hands. He also accused predecessor Hurlbut of operating a local liquor monopoly. Whiskey purchased at forty cents a gallon in Cincinnati was sold for seven dollars in Memphis.[20]

Later that year, Lincoln sent Major General Daniel Sickles, who had lost a leg at Gettysburg, to report on trade conditions in the lower Mississippi Valley. Sickles wrote that illicit trade was abundant: "Boats loaded with supplies have had almost unrestricted opportunities for trade on the Mississippi and some of its navigable tributaries, stopping everywhere along the river, and dealing with anybody." Historian William C. Harris concluded that if similar reports from Generals Banks, Edward R. S. Canby, and Washburn were valid, "the fall of Vicksburg and Port Hudson did not do the irreparable damage to the Confederate cause that historians have assumed." Harris reasoned that the increased cotton trade partially compensated for the loss of the fortifications by bringing in needed products.[21]

## Helena

Upon occupying Helena, Arkansas, in mid-July 1862, Union General Samuel Curtis complained that his camp was "infested with Jews, secessionists, and spies." By issuing orders that restricted trade to a few people he could control under military law as sutlers, Curtis adopted a policy that made him vulnerable to charges of improper monopolization. Shortly, a steady stream of rumored abuses percolated up to Chicago and the department headquarters for Curtis's army at St. Louis. Illinois senator Orville Browning's diary records Chicago rumors that Curtis deposited $150,000 with a Chicago financier less than three months after occupying Helena. Attorney General Edward Bates recorded similar hearsay in his diary, but the amount was $100,000.[22] Two months later, Browning met with an officer serving under Curtis who claimed that Curtis could have captured Little Rock and secured Arkansas for the Union but instead went to Helena because there was no cotton in Little Rock. By October 1862, the officer said, Curtis had already seized several million dollars worth of the fiber and "converted it to his own use."[23]

Later, Curtis wrote Lincoln directly to explain that the complaints originated out of envy from unsavory characters who were unworthy of trade privileges. Nonetheless, within a few months, the general was transferred to St. Louis to become the new department commander, and rumors of his possible fraud trailed along.

An investigating Treasury agent concluded that Helena's trade "diverted soldiers to become agents and brokers of cotton buying [and had] thrown thousands of dollars into the hands of our enemies." Corruption flourished at Helena, where the army had little to do during twelve months of idle occupation before invading central Arkansas in late summer 1863. Federal soldiers even purchased cotton from slaves with counterfeit Confederate money.[24] Nearby Union-loyal plantation owner James Alcorn secretly sold hundreds of bales of cotton, typically at nighttime, from vessels in the Mississippi River. He befriended federal officers in Helena and was rewarded with a pass to enter the town at will.[25]

Lincoln's military governor of Arkansas complained late in 1862 that the idle troops at Helena were principally engaged in profiting from cotton trade. They raided neighboring plantations to confiscate whatever cotton they could get. As an afterthought, they would often destroy the plantation homestead.[26] Helena's steady occupation led to deplorable sanitary conditions, particularly among the freed slaves who fled there. Yankee soldiers informally referred to the place as "Hell-in-Arkansas," as disease, malnutrition, and lack of clothes and shelter took a toll on the blacks who sought refuge in the town.[27]

Before the end of 1862, the inland federal navy began to get involved. Initially, Admiral David Dixon Porter sought to break up illegal trade. In time, however, he and his crews became covetous of cotton as a prize of war. Under maritime law, 50 percent of a captured cargo was subject to a reward for the crew of the ship making the capture. Five percent of the applicable half of the cargo was awarded to the crew seizing the prize. The prize fee was distributed among the sailors in amounts proportional to rank, with the captain getting the most. By the end of the war, Porter had become so aggressive at stealing cotton that Confederates gave him the nom de guerre Thief of the Mississippi. His sailors would seize bales and stencil "C.S.A" on them, thereby falsely representing the cotton as property of the Confederate government and therefore subject to prize law.[28] Historian Ludwell Johnson explained:

> According to an interpretation of . . . [naval] law . . . prizes might be taken wherever found. As a result, Federal gunboats in

> the Mississippi valley . . . [operated] to . . . [capture] cotton. 'Naval wagon trains' . . . would scour the country 10–15 miles back from the rivers and bring in large amounts of cotton to [divide] as lawful Naval prize. Many officers grew rich. Senator Chandler claimed that more than $100 million was realized . . . in this manner.[29]

Admiral David Dixon Porter. (*Library of Congress*)

William Kellogg, a former Illinois congressman and long-time Lincoln friend, tried to use the president's influence in a Helena cotton-trading scheme. When he outlined his plans to the president in June 1863, Lincoln told him he would have to clear them with Chase. But he gave Kellogg an endorsement to show to Chase, which concluded, "I wish [Kellogg] obliged so far as you can consistently do it." After quickly reading the note, Chase replied, "It cannot be done, sir." Ultimately, Kellogg's patronage award took the form of an appointment as chief justice of the Nebraska Territory early in 1865.[30]

Even after most of the federal army left Helena to capture Little Rock in autumn 1863, trade continued and may have even accelerated. In November, Rebel war clerk John B. Jones noted in his diary, "From [Helena] we have letters stating that all restraint is thrown off, and everybody almost is trading with the enemy. Some 1500 bales of cotton per week [are] taken to the Yankees from that region. They say most of the parties have permits from the government or from commanding generals to trade with the enemy."[31]

## New Orleans

Toward the end of 1861, General Butler asked then General in Chief George McClellan that he be given fifteen thousand troops to invade Texas. Butler's aim was to populate the Lone Star State with free immigrants in order to produce cheap cotton for New

England's textile mills. Butler was a Massachusetts Democratic politician and part owner of a textile plant. His interest in profiting from cotton trade predates even the first meaningful Union army victory, at Mill Springs, Kentucky, in January 1862.[32]

Butler raised an army in Massachusetts, but before it was deployed, Admiral Porter submitted a plan to capture New Orleans, which would be led by his foster brother, Admiral David Farragut. If successful, an occupation force would be required. Thus, Butler's army was diverted to the New Orleans venture in spring 1862.

After running past the downstream forts of St. Philip and Jackson as well as a modest Rebel flotilla, Farragut forced the surrender of New Orleans on April 25, 1862. Six days later, Butler occupied the Confederacy's largest city, where he would remain in command for about seven months. During that period he earned one of the most unsavory reputations of any Civil War general for self-serving economic activities that aided the enemy and damaged the military effort of his own side.

As a clever lawyer, Butler became increasingly skilled at covering his tracks. But instances early in the war when he was less cautious point to a corrupting pattern. For example, when Lincoln authorized him to raise an army of New Englanders, the methods used to recruit, supply, and transport his troops during the 1861–1862 winter provide an initial indication of the general's instincts to leverage his military status for personal profit. He began by populating his headquarters staff with family members and friends. Among them was older brother Andrew, unemployed brother-in-law Henry Read, and Richard Fay, who was treasurer of Middlesex Mills, where Butler was the chief shareholder. Fisher Hildreth was another brother-in-law lurking around who later became involved in numerous shady deals.[33]

In one early instance, a New York clothing supplier named Whipple met with Butler and Hildreth, offering to supply hats for fifteen dollars a dozen. Butler responded by asking, "can you let us have six thousand at your price, giving my quartermaster ten per cent to divide around?" Whipple declined, explaining that the general had "mistaken his man." A few months later, in January 1862, Whipple told Montgomery Meigs, who was quartermaster general for all Union armies, of the incident. Meigs asked that Whipple write a notarized accusation for him to present to Secretary of War Stanton. Whipple complied, and Meigs followed up with Stanton. Nothing further was done.[34]

General Benjamin Butler. (*Library of Congress*)

Transporting Butler's soldiers to New Orleans provided another profitable opportunity. Twenty ships were chartered. Circumstances involving at least three are disturbing.

In December 1861, two Northerners in the shipping business had a revealing conversation. A shipping clerk named Reed and a ship owner named White were meeting when Reed remarked that he had heard some of the ships Butler chartered were engaged under questionable terms. White, who owned one of the ships, wrote on a piece of paper "$4,000 a month" and underneath it wrote "$2,500 a month." He explained by pointing to the two numbers in sequence, "there [$4,000] is the way the charter party [i.e., contract] reads . . . ; there [$2,500] is what we get." Historian Ludwell Johnson concluded that such corrupted terms were standard Butler procedure. Participating ship owners were required to kickback a substantial portion of the monthly fee. When White was eventually called before an investigating committee of the US House, Johnson surmised that White was "remarkably forgetful, exceedingly evasive, and wholly disingenuous."[35]

In time, Butler's behavior earned him more powerful accusers. Among them was Massachusetts governor John Andrews, who complained repeatedly to Washington. Eventually the governor wrote the state's two senators, Charles Sumner and Henry Wilson, "I am compelled to . . . declare that the whole course of proceedings under Major General Butler in this Commonwealth seems to have been designed and adapted simply to afford means to persons of bad character to make money unscrupulously, and to encourage men whose unfitness had excluded them from any appointment by me."[36]

Butler arrived in New Orleans in May 1862 with personal capital of $150,000. Six years later his net worth was $3 million. The twentyfold increase could not have been achieved through salaries, dividends, and legal fees. Undoubtedly, the prime source was inter-belligerent trade and other corrupt practices during the war, chiefly at New Orleans, where brother Andrew was an accomplice.[37] Also involved was George Shepley, who was the military governor of Louisiana and later a collaborator with Butler in Norfolk, Virginia.[38] Author Chester Hearn wrote, "If anybody in the Treasury Department had paused to investigate the numerous transactions floating through the Lowell [Massachusetts] accounts of Fisher Hildreth and the Boston accounts of Richard S. Fay, Jr., they would have found the Butler brothers deeply immersed in transactions involving huge sums of money—but nobody did."[39]

Of the three captured Mississippi River trading centers, New Orleans held the most potential for intersectional commerce but was handicapped partly because General Butler alienated the local population. He hanged one citizen for slighting the American flag and threatened to arrest women who insulted Union soldiers in a disgusting manner.[40] More importantly, he gave his elder brother privileged controls, which were abused by bribery demands.[41] Consequently, trade volumes only grew slowly at first because many who were asked to pay bribes initially refused.

Nonetheless, within a few months, trading across enemy lines flourished in the Crescent City. Butler promised that planters who delivered bales into the city would not have them confiscated even if the owner were a high-ranking Confederate official.[42] When one British trader suggested that Butler permit cotton to be shipped to New Orleans from Confederate-controlled Mobile, Butler wrote the Rebel commander in Mobile offering to exchange salt for cotton. During the Civil War, salt was essential as a meat preservative.[43]

Because of a tightening cotton shortage in Britain and France, Secretary of State Seward sent a message to European diplomats in Washington four days after the occupation to notify them that the blockade at New Orleans would soon be lifted. He was implying that large quantities of cotton would quickly reach the market. Like Seward, Lincoln wanted to avoid a European cotton famine in order to minimize the chances that Britain and France might intervene in the war on the side of the Confederacy. Consequently, he was persuaded that Southern planters should be allowed to take their cotton into New Orleans, where it could be sold and not confiscated. In order to motivate Southerners to supply cotton, Butler went so far as to announce that produce (i.e., cotton, sugar, etc.) could be sold for specie.

Butler immediately began attempts to participate in the lucrative trade. He used a federal warship to send $60,000 in sugar to Boston, where he expected to sell it for $160,000. However, his use of the government ship was reported. Instead of his earning a profit, military authorities only permitted him to recover his $60,000 plus expenses. Thereafter, his brother Andrew officially represented the family in such transactions. Everyone in New Orleans believed that Andrew accumulated a profit of $1million to $2 million while in Louisiana. On inquiry from Treasury Secretary Chase in October 1862, the general responded that his brother actually cleared less than $200,000.[44]

An example of the corrupting influence of intersectional wartime trade is the story of young George Denison, who was assigned to keep an eye on the Butler brothers. After New Orleans was captured, Secretary Chase appointed Denison, a twenty-nine-year-old relative of his, as the new customs collector to replace the one previously reporting to the Confederate government. Denison was a graduate of the University of Vermont and an abolitionist. A few years earlier, Denison had married a Southern girl who later died in childbirth. When the war started, he was in Texas managing her estate, which ironically included about seventy slaves.

Denison arrived in New Orleans in July 1862 and promptly began writing Chase weekly, reporting suspicious commerce involving General Butler's friends and his brother Andrew. As noted, Louisiana's military governor, George Shepley, was among the friends. When Denison discovered illegal shipments of salt to Confederates across Lake Pontchartrain, he seized one of the vessels. General Butler had the ship released because it had a permit. Denison learned that Shepley issued such passes on demand for Butler, although he suspected that requests normally originated with the general's brother.[45]

Shamefully, less than six months after arriving in New Orleans, Denison himself was taking bribes. He met with General Nathaniel Banks when he replaced Butler in December 1862 to tell the newcomer that as special agent for the Treasury Department, Denison held exclusive authority in all matters of trade within the region. During the preceding months, businessmen often found it perplexingly difficult to secure legally entitled permits of various types until they learned to present Denison with a cash gift. It was a classic case of power inducing corruption. Although Denison was soon replaced, he was never punished. At the end of the war, he was a member of a partnership leasing three cotton plantations. He died of illness before the end of 1865, on a voyage back to the Northeast.[46]

Unfortunately for the Union, fewer than thirty thousand cotton bales were officially exported from New Orleans during the first five months of occupation, compared to the monthly rate of one hundred sixty-five thousand prior to the war, translating to a 95 percent decline. Despite Treasury regulations, General Butler tightly controlled trade authorizations. Brother Andrew sometimes enjoyed monopolies, which could be used to block proposals that failed to profit his interests, which was one reason for the initially slow pace of trade recovery in the city.[47]

Shortly before being recalled to Washington, Butler made an audacious proposal to the agent of a plantation owner named Stevenson. It was so remarkable that Stevenson described it in a letter to the Confederate secretary of war. Butler offered to let planters haul cotton into New Orleans and transship it to any port in the world. Stevenson explained that when the cotton arrived at its destination, the monetary value of the cargo could be deposited to the credit of the Confederate government at most any reputable banking institution. According to a Confederate War Department clerk, Stevenson went so far as to proclaim, "Butler will let us have *anything* for a bribe."[48]

Soon after the Second Confiscation Act became effective in September 1862, General Butler increasingly relied on it as a means of seizing cotton. Since the act permitted confiscation of property owned by anyone aiding the Confederacy, Butler reversed his earlier method of encouraging trade, which was to refrain from confiscating cotton voluntarily brought into New Orleans for sale. Instead, after the Second Confiscation Act, he started grabbing whatever cotton or other "Rebel" property he could get his hands on.

First he conducted a census in which the four thousand respondents failing to pledge loyalty to the Union were banished and their property seized. Confiscated articles were sold at ridiculously low auction prices where Andrew was often the prime buyer. Next the general sent expeditions into the countryside with no purpose other than to confiscate cotton from residents assumed to be disloyal. Once brought into New Orleans, the cotton was similarly sold in rigged auctions. To maintain correct appearances, auction proceeds were dutifully held for the benefit of "just claimants," but the Butler consortium still ended up owning the cotton at bargain prices because it was the buyer. (One way a cotton owner might be a "just claimant" would be to prove that the cotton was illegally confiscated because he or she was a Union-loyal citizen.) Later it would sell its accumulated inventories at much higher market prices. Butler "sequestered" (i.e., made vulnerable to confiscation) such "properties" in all of Louisiana beyond parishes surrounding New Orleans.[49]

Interbelligerent trade in the Mississippi Valley was demoralizing to soldiers of both armies, but especially those of the Union. The profit motive was corrupting. Although army property was ordinarily not used for transporting cotton, army and navy officers could be bribed to make increasingly common exceptions. One investigator claimed that nearly every officer was in partnership with a cotton trader, while every soldier hoped to add a cotton bale to his monthly pay. Such attitudes spread like an infectious disease. A federal officer at occupied Memphis stated bluntly, "The . . . system of trade has given strength to the Rebel army while it has demoralized and weakened our own."[50]

The corruption on the Union side was so widespread that even the Confederates commented on it. One remarked that Major General John McArthur, commanding at Vicksburg (after it was captured by Grant in July 1863), required a bribe in order to permit bales from Rebel plantations to pass through the town to the riverfront docks. He would also delay military expeditions into nearby areas if suppliers of cotton were not yet ready to deliver their bales to Vicksburg. In this manner he prevented such cotton from being confiscated. As cotton traders passed through the lines, they not only provided Confederates with supplies but also military intelligence, including anticipated Union troop movements.[51]

## Banks Replaces Butler

After the 1862 congressional elections resulted in Republican setbacks in the Northwest the president concluded that opening the Mississippi River to commercial navigation was more important than capturing Texas lands that might be turned over to Northerners to grow cotton.[52] Simultaneously, Lincoln decided to replace Butler with General Banks because of the former's lack of military progress and the steady rumors of his fiscal improprieties.

It was a bitter pill for Butler, who hated his replacement partly as a result of narrowly losing an election for Massachusetts governor to him shortly before the war. Within two weeks of arriving in mid-December, Banks received, but did not accept, the following proposal from Andrew Butler and one of his associates:

> Dear Sir:
>
> If you will allow our commercial program to be [carried?] out as projected previous to your arrival in this department, giving the same support . . . as your predecessor, I am authorized to place at your disposal $100,000.[53]

General Nathaniel Banks. (*Library of Congress*)

Upon arriving in New Orleans, Banks immediately suspended all sales of sequestered property. The following month he announced that no further property would be seized except by his order. Two months later he proclaimed that all commercial transactions must use US Treasury notes (greenbacks), thereby forbidding gold payments. He was criticized by the many speculators arriving with his army. They expected him to take the army into Texas to capture cotton lands. Failing in that, they expected that he would at least adopt policies to facilitate between-the-lines commerce in Louisiana. However, his initial steps, like the greenback requirement, actually made such trade more difficult by discouraging sellers. Although Banks proposed a mission into upstate Louisiana to seize cotton under terms granting half the value to the growers as an incentive to refrain from their self-destruction of it, General in Chief Halleck reminded him that his prime objective was to clear the Mississippi River.

Despite the improved morality of Banks's military administration, Louisiana corruption could not be eradicated. As will be discussed in a later chapter, after the last of the Rebel fortifications on the Mississippi River were cleared, Banks made a final major effort to secure cotton for his New England constituency by advancing up the Red River. Although Butler was recalled to Washington, his presence was a problem for Lincoln because the general was popular among radical Republicans who were offended by his removal. They particularly appreciated his novel legal interpretation, which had become an accepted convention, of classifying escaped slaves as "contraband of war" and therefore ineligible to be returned to their owners.

The radicals also admired his iron-fisted control of New Orleans, including the command to treat disrespectful females as "women of the street plying their trade," thereby earning him the sobriquet "Beast" Butler. Like Butler himself, his supporters seemed to be proud that prominent Southerners had put a price on his head and that Jefferson Davis said Butler's crimes merited capital punishment if he was ever captured. Consequently, when offered a command farther up the Mississippi River, he declined, saying he would consider nothing less than a return to New Orleans. But if he had accepted the upriver job, it may have been Butler instead of Grant who would have been assigned responsibility to capture Vicksburg—a mission for which he had dubious ability.[54]

## Federal Plantations

As a consequence of meager cotton production and the Confederate practice of burning inventories threatened with capture by an advancing enemy, the Union soon began efforts to grow cotton on seized plantations in the Mississippi Valley, much as was done earlier in Port Royal. The policy was also triggered by a Northern aversion to receiving black refugees. For example, Horace Greely's prominent opposition to slavery did not extend so far as to endorse racial integration in his neighborhood. His *New York Tribune* advocated that occupied Southern lands be given to ex-slaves in order to avoid mass black migration into the North.[55] As explained by Adjutant General Lorenzo Thomas after Lincoln sent him into the Mississippi Valley in spring 1863 to recruit African-American soldiers and develop a system that would industriously employ the remaining former slaves in cotton production:

> It will not do to send [black refugees] . . . into the free states, for the prejudices of the people of those states are against such a measure and some . . . have enacted laws against the reception of free negroes. . . . [Former slaves] are coming in upon us in such numbers that some provision must be made for them. You cannot send them North. You all know the prejudices of the Northern people against receiving large numbers of the colored race. Look upon the river and see the multitude of deserted plantations upon its banks. These are the places for those freedmen.[56]

General Lorenzo Thomas. (*Library of Congress*)

The process began earlier near New Orleans after the city became crowded with runaway slaves following its capture in April 1862. Six months later, General Butler started allowing Union-loyal planters in adjacent parishes to use ex-slaves to work their fields in exchange for wages. When Banks took over from Butler in December 1862, he extended the practice throughout occupied Louisiana, insisting that former slaves must avoid vagrancy and idleness.[57]

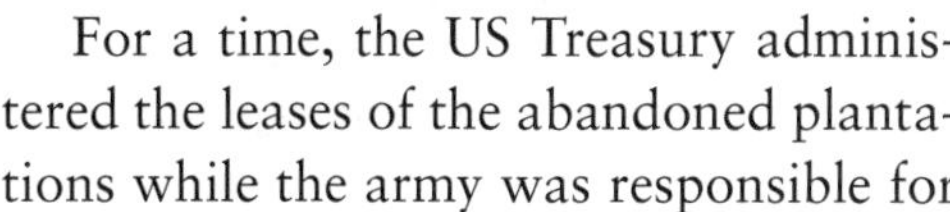

For a time, the US Treasury administered the leases of the abandoned plantations while the army was responsible for policing the labor contracts on them, but eventually full control went to the army. Although planters were forbidden to flog their workers, military authorities were allowed to whip those who refused to work. The army also provided patrolling guards to keep laborers from leaving the plantations until their contracts expired. One African-American newspaper in New Orleans protested, "Any white man subjected to such restrictive and humiliating prohibitions would certainly call himself a slave."[58]

By May 1863, when Grant had Vicksburg under siege and Banks encircled Port Hudson, numerous abandoned plantations along the lower Mississippi became available for lease, including 136 near Vicksburg. White Northerners, who were sometimes former army officers, leased about 85 percent of them, with the remaining 15 percent taken by former slaves. Additionally, about thirty plantations in the area continued to be operated by Southerners willing to take a loyalty oath to the Union.[59]

Although terms varied over the next two years because of changing government regulations, they were typically as follows: Lessees paid a two-dollar-per-bale tax. Wage rates for ex-slaves were seven dollars monthly for men over age fifteen and five dollars for women in the same age bracket. Children twelve to fifteen were paid half wages, and those under twelve were exempt from fieldwork. Employment contracts required laborers to work an entire season, putting in ten hours daily in the summer and nine in the winter. Opportunistic white Northerners flooded into the delta. New York journalist Thomas W. Knox wrote, "The majority of the lessees were unprincipled men, who undertook the enterprise solely as speculation. They had as little regard for the rights of the Negro as the most brutal slaveholder. . . . Some . . . made an open boast of having swindled their Negroes out of their summers wages."[60]

A War Department survey suggests that the apparent promise of quick cotton riches attracted undesirable, inexperienced, and underproductive freebooters from the North. Specifically it concluded that the "old planters [were] dealing fairly with the freedmen . . . [and] have paid them more promptly, more justly and apparently with more willingness than new lessees." The Southern planters who remained took a longer-term view. They were primarily concerned with earning a living and holding onto their property until the return of peace and civil government.[61]

Lorenzo Thomas encouraged family and friends to lease plantations, especially near Natchez, Mississippi, where the general enjoyed cordial relations with leading citizens dating from before the war. He hired publicity agents to entice Northerners into his leasing program. One advertised a return of $15,000 on a $2,000 investment. The general may himself have had an interest in his son Henry's rented plantation in Concordia Parish, Louisiana, directly across the Mississippi River from Natchez. For a time, one of the commissioners in charge of plantation leasing under the Thomas plan was Judge Lewis Dent, who was General Ulysses Grant's father-in-law. When journalist Knox and a partner decided to get into the plantation-leasing business, they discovered "that the best plantations in the Natchez area had been taken by the friends of Adjutant General Thomas."[62]

Many newcomers discovered it was difficult to profit by growing cotton. One wrote to the *Wisconsin State Journal* with a number of complaints, including the necessity to pay bribes. "Who hath much greenbacks and expected more? The official that letteth the plantation." Bribes of $1,500 were commonly required by Treasury agents to facilitate cotton transportation because of excessive red tape involving affidavits of contract fulfillment, proofs of origin for the cotton, and other procedural obstacles. Provost marshals sometimes required bribes in order to fulfill their duties to police and discipline the freedmen. The Wisconsin writer also complained of ineffective military protection from Rebel guerrillas and the impressment of his own horses and mules by Union soldiers as well as recruiting agents from the North taking his workers when seeking black males as draft substitutes for Northern whites wanting to avoid military service.[63]

Confederate guerrillas frustrated a consortium of Northerners leasing twenty thousand acres in northeast Louisiana. After a series of raids, the Yankees agreed to evacuate the land in July 1864 if the Southerners would finish cultivating and marketing the crop in exchange for half of the proceeds. It was evidently the best arrangement that could be negotiated because the Union provost guards in nearby Vicksburg, who would normally protect the leased lands, seemed to be on poker-playing terms with some of the raiders.[64]

In contrast to the poor financial results plaguing many white lessees, Knox discovered that some of the former slaves who operated their own farms earned good profits. Although only able to lease much smaller properties, they benefitted from experience and high wartime cotton prices. Ten near Helena earned $31,000 in a year. Two planted forty acres and each cleared almost $7,000. Another leased twenty-four acres and cleared over $4,000.[65]

While government-leased plantations productively employed many former slaves, the initiative did little to satisfy the raw-material appetite of the textile industry. As may be observed from Table 1 in chapter 1, cotton production in the Southern states dropped 70 percent in 1863 and 33 percent in 1864. Partly owing to the devastating impact of a pestilence of armyworms, about 90 percent of 1864 lessees returned home without renewing their leases the following year. Although cotton production rebounded sharply to two million bales in 1865 from three hundred thousand in 1864, the gain principally resulted from widespread farming by former Confederate soldiers who returned to peacetime activities.[66]

Although started during the war, plantation leasing became a standard practice when peace was restored. It enabled former slave-holding planters to avoid breaking up their large land tracts into small parcel sales. It also provided a complementary benefit to most Northern investors who were not interested in living in the South but hoped to make a quick killing in the cotton market. Renting enabled them to pursue such goals without tying up capital in illiquid real estate investments. One prominent example was William Sprague, who leased thirteen plantations along the Mississippi River shortly after General Lee's surrender at Appomattox on April 9, 1865. But after only a year, the senator learned it was harder to earn a profit than he realized, and he closed the venture.[67]

*Six*

# Abusing the Blockade

FIFTEEN DAYS AFTER THE BOMBARDMENT OF FORT SUMTER, President Lincoln extended the blockade to all of the Confederacy's coastal states, including North Carolina, which had not then seceded. As noted, terms of the 1856 Paris Declaration of Maritime Law permitted signatories, which included most European powers, to officially declare neutrality and grant belligerency rights to both the North and South. Consequently, the Richmond government could buy arms and equipment from neutrals. Belligerency status also permitted the South to raise foreign loans and afforded it rights of search and seizure, thereby paving the way for seagoing commerce raiders such as the CSS *Alabama* and CSS *Shenandoah*.[1]

Initially the United States had few ships with which to enforce the blockade. At the start of the war, the navy had about one hundred vessels, but only thirty-four were steamers, and some of those were merely tenders.[2] Furthermore, the navy was not even able to station the available ships off the major Southern ports until July 1861. Even then the blockade was paper thin. Therefore, deep-water ships from Europe could often slip into Rebel ports, but most such vessels were wind-powered because the room required by engines and coal reduced storage space. Since sail-driven ships depended on unpredictable winds, it was almost impossible for them to escape the pursuit of a blockading steamer. Therefore, by the end of the first year of the war, it was necessary to develop another way to get cargoes into the Confederacy.

Deep-water vessels began carrying their cargoes from Europe (or even New York and Boston) to selected neutral ports closer to the Confederacy, such as Nassau in the Bahamas, St. George in Bermuda, and Havana. As will be explained shortly, Halifax was an exceptional and more-distant example. Typically, fast, shallow-draft steamers conveyed cargoes on the final leg from the neutral ports into the major harbors of the Confederacy. Small sailing vessels were also often used, but they normally traveled between the neutral harbors and secondary locations on the Rebel coastline not effectively blockaded.

Eventually, Wilmington, North Carolina, became the chief Rebel port, although Charleston, South Carolina, was the leader until September 1863, when the defenses on Morris Island became untenable and were abandoned. Wilmington, about six hundred miles from Nassau and seven hundred from Bermuda, could be reached from either port in two to three days. The town was guarded by powerful Fort Fisher, twenty-five miles downstream at the mouth of the Cape Fear River. Charleston was defended by Fort Sumter, other fortifications, and a number of innovative nautical weapons, including the CSS *Hunley*, which made the world's first successful submarine attack by sinking the USS *Housatonic* in February 1864. Havana principally served the gulf coast ports of New Orleans, Galveston, Mobile, and Matamoros. But the federals captured New Orleans only a year after Fort Sumter, and Mobile fell a little more than two years later. Galveston and Matamoros were far from the Confederacy's main population centers. Although Bermuda was more distant than Nassau from both Wilmington and Charleston, some blockade-runners preferred it because the island was more difficult for the federal blockading fleets to patrol owing to its distance from Union-friendly refueling depots.

During the first half of the war, Nassau was the leading transshipping site for blockade-running. Between 1861 and 1865, four

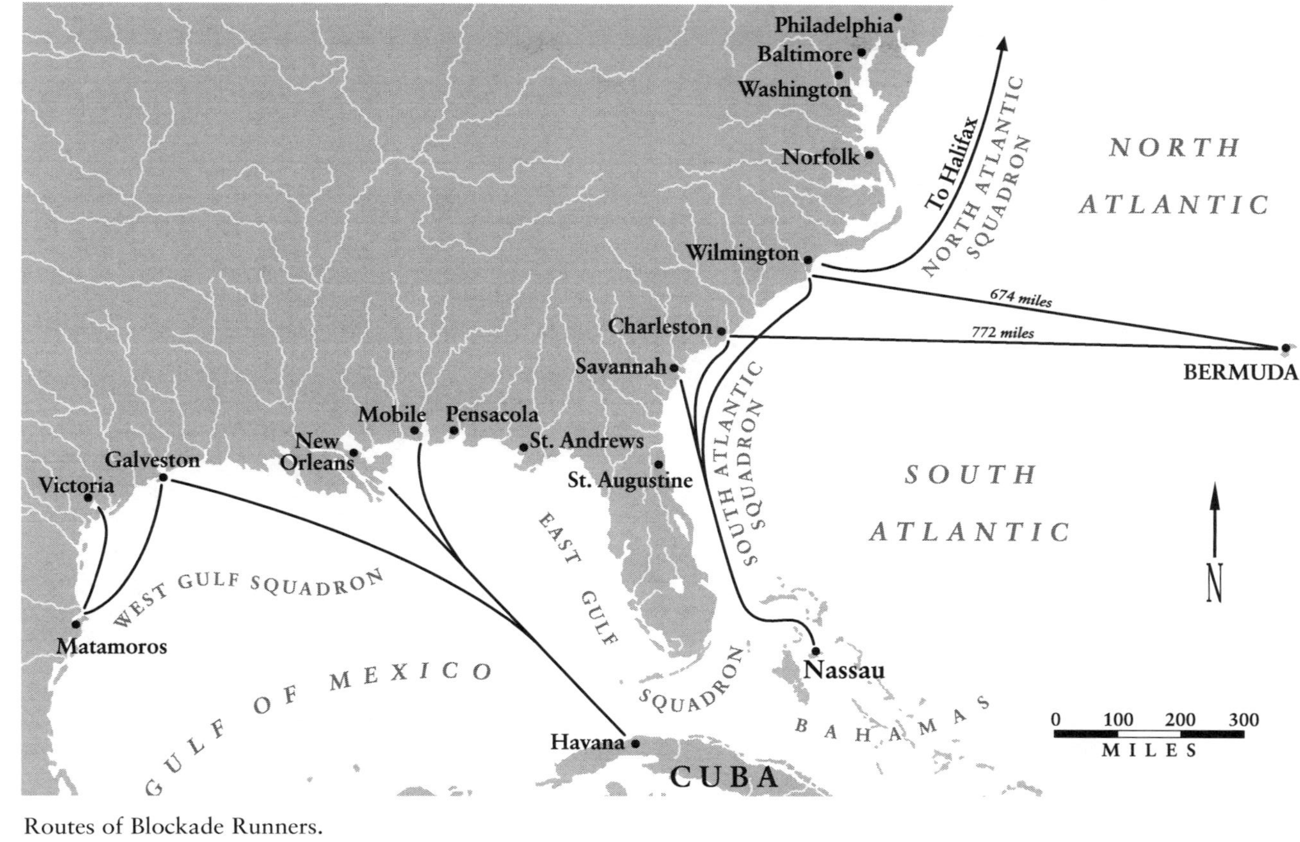


Routes of Blockade Runners.

hundred vessels entered Nassau from the Confederacy, and almost six hundred departed for the Southern states, although two-thirds were officially cleared for other destinations. The war transformed the community like the prince's kiss did Sleeping Beauty. For a few brief years, dollars were spent like pennies, and the previously obscure British colony was converted into a boomtown. But Nassau became less popular in the second half of the war because of yellow-fever outbreaks there and its closer proximity to Union-blockading squadrons as compared to Bermuda, which emerged as the principal blockade-running center in the second half of the war.[3]

While many of the cargoes destined for the Confederacy originated in Europe, some came from Northern states. One example was anthracite coal from Pennsylvania, which was preferred as a way to minimize the telltale smoke of runners attempting to sneak past the federal blockade. After the fall of Vicksburg, one researcher concluded that most of the meat sustaining Lee's army in 1864 was originally from New York, transshipped via Nassau. Since it sometimes arrived in a spoiled condition, authorities in Richmond facetiously suggested they needed to station a meat inspector in New York.[4] On visiting Nassau a year after the war started, the British consul in Charleston wrote the British minister to Lincoln's government, Lord Lyons:

> The blockade-runners are doing a great business. . . . The Richmond government sent about a month ago an order to Nassau for medicine, quinine, etc. It went from Nassau to New York, was executed there, came back to Nassau, thence here, and was on its way to Richmond in 21 days from the date of the order. Nearly all the trade is under the British flag. The vessels are all changed in Nassau and Havana. Passengers come and go freely and no one seems to think there is the slightest risk—which indeed there is not.[5]

More than one hundred blockade-runners were built in England over the nearly three years from early 1862 to late 1864. They were typically 180 feet long, with a 22-foot beam, and propelled by side-mounted paddlewheels that required less draft than a propeller ship. The ships were painted in dull colors to make them difficult to spot. The typical crew was British, because neutrals were not imprisoned if captured. In a round trip, a skipper could earn $5,000 in gold, whereas the pilot and engineer were paid $2,500 and the average crewman $250.[6]

Although even farther from important Confederate harbors than Bermuda, Nassau, or Havana, the anchorage at Halifax also gained a blockade-running reputation, for two reasons.

First, a technicality of the transshipment process enabled merchants in the United States to circumvent restrictions against selling products into the Confederacy. Specifically, US-flagged ships could legally enter Canadian ports and unload cargo, thereby converting the freight into Canadian goods. The same ships could then reload the cargoes and take them to Bermuda or Nassau, where they could be sold to buyers who would freight them into the Confederacy on blockade-runners. On the return trip the process would be reversed, with the result that incongruous "Canadian" cotton was legally imported into the United States.

Although proper under US law, the subterfuge was cumbersome. In time many skippers merely used fake papers, which declared that one cargo had been unloaded at Halifax and another loaded. Sometimes such ships never went to Halifax at all, but instead traveled directly from US ports to Bermuda or Nassau with their captains carrying papers falsely representing that the vessels first went to Halifax.[7] Secretary of State Seward's son and assistant, Fred, claimed that the Halifax trading firms of B. Weir & Company, G. C. Harvey, Alexander Keith, and S. F. Barss, among others, were "willing agents and abettors of enemies of the United States."[8]

A second reason for using Halifax became evident in 1864, when Nassau suffered a yellow fever outbreak. During the war, yellow fever was a deadly disease that led Confederate port authorities to quarantine ships arriving from locations with serious outbreaks. Such quarantines were time consuming and reduced the number of runs an affected ship could make in a fixed time period compared to ships that were not delayed by quarantine.[9]

Among the items that skipped Canada and went directly from the United States to "neutral" buyers in Nassau or Bermuda, preserved meat was particularly valuable. A favorite was "Bermuda Bacon." Buyers would simply visit hog farmers in New York and nearby states and offer far more per pound for hams and bacon than the US government or civilian merchants were offering. The large supplies of pork products were salted and shipped out of New York or Philadelphia to Bermuda or Nassau. This was especially true during the first years of the war.

No one seemed to wonder why the people of these islands were suddenly eating vast quantities of pork. Upon arrival in the islands, the hams and bacon were sold at quadruple their cost to agents of the Confederate commissary, then shipped to hungry soldiers on the firing line.[10]

But provisions and preserved meats were not all that was being shipped from the United States to blockade-running centers. Weapons were sometimes included, as in the case of a shipload of pistols from Boston hidden in barrels of lard.[11] Instances were discovered of munitions concealed in trunks taken on board in New York and cannon shipped in boxes labeled "hardware."[12]

In 1863, Wilmington merchants told a young Confederate soldier passing through town that some cargoes arrived directly from New York. The judge advocate for the South Atlantic Blockading Squadron wrote, "We have been accustomed to berate . . . Great Britain for exporting goods to the Confederacy. But probably more goods were carried into the Confederate States by merchants of the United States than all [those] of Europe. The munitions of war were furnished in very large quantities to the enemies of the United States by the citizens of the United States."[13] Direct trade between Northeastern American ports and the Bahamas, Bermuda, and Cuba doubled during the Civil War. Virtually all cargo going into those places from the United States ended up in the Confederacy.[14]

Shops at Bermuda featured shoes and other articles from Connecticut and Massachusetts labeled "London," felt hats from New York tagged "Paris," and "Irish" whisky from New Jersey.[15] Major Norman S. Walker, a Confederate agent in Bermuda, regu-

The former Confederate blockade runner *Robert E. Lee* off Norfolk, Virginia, in December 1864. (*Library of Congress*)

larly bought contraband supplies from New York. Most of it was sent to Wilmington, which was the chief port supplying General Lee's Army of Northern Virginia. On June 17, 1863, the American consul at St. George wrote Secretary of State Seward, "I beg to apprise you that large quantities of merchandise are shipped from New York to these islands and here transshipped on board steamers for blockade ports. There is no doubt that Major Walker who styles himself as a Confederate States agent is receiving goods [from] New York by almost every vessel. . . . A large proportion of the goods shipped from here to Wilmington are from New York."[16]

In Chesapeake Bay, vessels cleared from New York, Philadelphia, and Baltimore for Washington, DC, would simply stop on the way to discharge cargo in Tidewater Virginia. Other cargoes shipped to Norfolk were transshipped via canals to North Carolina's Albemarle Sound. From there they could be taken up rivers into Virginia to supply Lee's army.[17]

As Lee was preparing for the invasion of Pennsylvania, Confederate War Department clerk Jones wrote in his famous diary on June 8, 1863, "the arrival and departure of steamers amount to one per day and most of the imported goods are of Yankee manufacture." Most of the illicit trade originated in New York. Although US customs procedures involving certificates of clearance and monetary bonds were established in an attempt to ensure that contraband cargoes did not end up in the Confederacy, bribery was commonly employed to defraud the paperwork requirements.[18]

Secretary Chase had granted customs officers the authority to force shippers in the United States carrying freight to Nassau or Bermuda to post a bond equal to the value of the cargo. The bond was to be forfeited if it was discovered that the cargoes were intended for blockade-runners. But the plan fell victim to loopholes and bribery. For some reason, Baltimore and Philadelphia discontinued the bond requirements shortly after New York became more insistent on them. Furthermore, New York shippers often claimed to be British citizens, although they may only have been conduits paid a bribe to fraudulently conceal the true American cargo or ship owner. US-flagged ships changed registry, not only to avoid vulnerability to Confederate commerce raiders such as the CSS *Alabama* but to sidestep the bond requirements for cargoes carried in American hulls.

One way for shippers to cut through the red tape was to "buy back" the bond from a dishonest customs agent. The Henry B. Stanton family was a good example. Stanton was a noted abolitionist, and his wife, Elizabeth, was a leading feminist. Henry and his son, Neil, secured lucrative sinecures as customs agents. The younger Stanton readily admitted that he would sell bonds back to shippers. In one case he enabled a shipper to avoid liability for a $64,000 bond by selling it back to him for $600. Thus the shipper could send the cargo to a Confederate agent in Nassau or Bermuda without concern that his bond might be forfeited. Secretary Chase launched an investigation of the Stantons in October 1863, and Henry resigned a couple of months later. It was a significant setback that would lead to Chase's downfall the following summer as he battled Seward and Thurlow Weed for the privilege to assign patronage jobs in New York customs, where the majority of duties were collected.[19]

Perhaps most stunning of all were the Northern shippers who exported merchandise directly into Southern ports. It was easy enough to enter Union-occupied ports such as New Orleans and Beaufort, South Carolina, but some Yankee shippers would run the blockade of Rebel harbors without even attempting to use the middlemen available in Nassau, Bermuda, Havana, or Halifax. Because it was smuggling it was done secretly, so there will never be reliable statistics, but there is evidence that it was substantial. For example, Admiral Farragut was opposed to capturing Mobile until an occupation force could be made available because "the whole of Rebeldom would be supplied through it by our own people."[20]

Richmond war clerk Jones's diary provides further evidence that direct trade between ports in the Confederacy and others in the United States was more common than recognized in popular history. In June 1863, he wrote that most of the steamers at Wilmington were "filled with Yankee goods." In spring 1863, he learned that selected shippers in Mobile were sending cargoes directly to Union-occupied New Orleans. In May 1863, he wrote that many ships leaving Wilmington steered directly for New York once they cleared the harbor.[21]

In January 1864, his diary records that a trader in Mobile has "authority from the United States . . . to trade anything but arms and ammunition for cotton." A March 1864 diary entry notes that a Savannah resident had five steamers available to run the blockade and could "easily make arrangements with the Federal commandant at Fort Pulaski to let them pass and re-pass." In October of the same year, the diary states that a Confederate agent in Canada reached an agreement with a New York dealer to supply the Confederate government with bacon on terms bartering bacon pound-for-pound for cotton. During January 1865, he wrote that the Confederate Treasury secretary sold cotton to "Yankees" for gold and used the monetary metal to purchase Confederate paper money on the open market in order to improve currency quotations.[22]

On at least one occasion, a blockade-runner carried authorization directly from President Lincoln. In August 1864, he gave a permit to Texas military governor Andrew Jackson Hamilton, "or any person authorized in writing by him," to ship cotton through the blockade at either Galveston or Sabine Pass. The bales were to be delivered to a Treasury agent in New Orleans, where they would be sold at auction with 75 percent of the proceeds turned over to Hamilton and his partners. Lincoln's permit advised Major General Canby in charge at New Orleans and Admiral Farragut commanding the applicable blockade squadron that "the passage of [Hamilton's] vessels and cargos shall not be molested or hindered." Farragut complained to Navy Secretary Welles, who confronted the president. After a time of attempting to deflect responsibility to Secretary of State Seward, Lincoln revoked Hamilton's permit.[23]

Hamilton's proposition coincided with a surge in Texas blockade-running. Earlier in the war, steamers seldom bothered with the Texas ports because they were too distant from the major markets east of the Mississippi River, and the extra coal required to reach them reduced shipboard cargo space. By summer 1864, the blockade fleets east of the Mississippi were much larger. Consequently, a runner's probability of capture was much greater than earlier. By comparison, the fleets off Texas ports like Galveston and Sabine Pass were mere token blockades. In August and September 1864, three steamers tested the Galveston market after leaving Havana. When all three returned safely to Cuba, their crews reported that Texas Confederates had an abundant supply of low-priced cotton. Furthermore, the Rebels were so hungry for military and other supplies that incoming cargoes could be sold at much higher prices than in harbors east of the Mississippi. Kirby Smith's Cotton Bureau (to be discussed later) purchased most of the imports.[24]

While few US citizens were convicted of shipping goods into the Confederacy from the North, there is little doubt that the profits were big enough to enable violators to pay bribes in order to evade justice. For example, in June 1863, one government investigator introduced himself to suspected New York blockade-runner John Moore. The investigator represented himself as a Confederate agent seeking a way to send a shipment to Virginia. Moore struck a deal with a local captain named Benedict, who agreed to carry the cargo.

Benedict and Moore were arrested but escaped punishment by order of Assistant Secretary of War Thomas Scott.[25]

Shipments from Chesapeake Bay often reached North Carolina's Albemarle Sound by way of the Dismal Swamp Canal with the connivance of Treasury agents and military officers. Cargoes were shipped from the sound up the Chowan and other rivers into Virginia.[26] After the fall of Fort Fisher in January 1865, Lee's army was supplied almost entirely by trade via this route until March 8, 1865, when Lincoln yielded to protests by Grant to put a stop to it by enabling the general to discontinue permits and cancel those already issued east of the Appalachians. It was a matter of some embarrassment to Lincoln, who commented to his bodyguard, Ward Hill Lamon, "I wonder when General Grant changed his mind on this subject. He was the first man, after the commencement of the war, to grant a permit for the passage of cotton through the lines, and that to his own father."[27]

Estimates for the number of blockade-runs completed during the war vary widely, since unreported smugglers were also blockade-runners. Historian Frank Owsley put the figure at eighty-two hundred, including sailing vessels and steamers.[28] Author Stephen R. Wise estimated that steamers alone attempted thirteen hundred runs, with nearly an 80 percent success rate.[29]

Ruins of the naval dock at Norfolk, Virginia, destroyed by the Confederates in 1861. (*Library of Congress*)

*Seven*

# Norfolk

IN LATE SPRING 1862, WHEN MAJOR GENERAL GEORGE B. McClellan launched his campaign to capture Richmond from the southeast by marching up the peninsula between the York and James rivers, the Confederates were forced to abandon Norfolk and nearby areas. After dueling the ironclad USS *Monitor* to a draw several months earlier, the armored ram CSS *Virginia* was scuttled. It drew too much water to move to a safe anchorage farther upstream. By the end of June 1862, the federals occupied Norfolk and a surrounding region encompassing a population of about forty thousand.[1]

McClellan's one-hundred-thousand-man army blocked Norfolk civilians from obtaining supplies from the Confederacy. If the civilians were to survive, it would be necessary for the federal military forces to make allowances for Norfolk-area citizens to trade with others outside the region. Because Norfolk was a blockaded port, the 1856 Paris Declaration of Maritime Law, which was the Lincoln-Seward basis of the federal blockade, required that it be opened for trade from any neutral country once it became a Union-occupied city.

## Major General John Dix

However, sixty-four-year-old Major General John Dix, who was the occupation commander, did not want the blockade lifted. Rather, he desired to be given the authority to grant permits to individual businessmen, empowering them to import and export merchandise in sufficient quantities to sustain the area's economy. Essentially, he was reaching for monopolistic control over trade into and out of Norfolk.

Dix was a New York businessman and politician with connections to powerful characters who might be described as "robber barons" in the soon-to-arrive Gilded Age. In the final months of the Buchanan administration, Dix was secretary of the Treasury. His appointment was a gesture to a Wall Street community that was losing confidence in the Union during the secession crisis and threatening to discontinue bond purchases needed to finance government operations. The month before Dix's appointment, the federal government was unable to float a $5 million issue, even at a 12 percent interest rate. His predecessor supported the evacuation of Fort Sumter in order to avoid open warfare. New York financiers told Buchanan that they wanted such a man replaced by another who held strong Union credentials and suggested Dix. In 1853, he became president of the Mississippi & Missouri Railroad, which was to become an integral link across Iowa for the first transcontinental railroad. After the war, he was president of the Union Pacific Railroad during its scandalous construction phase. He was an ally of New York political boss Thurlow Weed's, who had earlier promoted legislation for the formation of the New York Central Railroad, which was the largest American corporation of its day.[2]

Along with Nathaniel Banks, John C. Frémont, and Benjamin Butler, Dix was one of Lincoln's four most prominent "political" generals. All four attempted to use their military positions to political advantage, while Butler and Dix also leveraged them for personal economic gain. The varied appointments over his career suggest that Dix was a skilled logroller and influence peddler.

At Norfolk, he first asked that Secretary of War Stanton request trading permits from Treasury Secretary Chase. Chase directed customs collectors at Boston, New York, Philadelphia, and Baltimore to grant limited permits to "reliable persons" for authorization to carry cargoes to and from Norfolk. One such permit went to a protégée of Hiram Barney's who managed Chase's New York real estate holdings and loaned the Treasury secretary $45,000, which may have never been repaid. Barney was also a Treasury customs collector whose duties included receiving and selling confiscated cotton from the Confederacy for a 5 percent fee.[3]

General John Dix. (*Library of Congress*)

However, since Chase had presidential ambitions and wanted to avoid even the appearance of impropriety, he required that Stanton certify the shipments were a "military necessity." As the summer wore on, trade in Dix's department grew rapidly. Stanton was letting Dix originate some of the certificates. But despite the growth, Dix wanted more volume and needed a way to eliminate "military necessity" as a restriction. His ambition was setting him up for a confrontation with the blockade policy of Navy Secretary Gideon Welles.[4]

Originally, the blockade at Norfolk was under the direction of Rear Admiral Louis Goldsborough, who was amenable to Dix's arrangements. However, Rear Admiral Samuel Lee soon replaced Goldsborough. Thus began a war-within-a-war as Dix and Welles fought a battle of words and letters. Welles took the position that Norfolk was still under blockade since Lincoln had not yet declared the port open for business. While Dix liked the idea of blockading everyone else, he wanted *his* ships to pass through under the authority of permits. Essentially, Welles responded that he did not care about permits. So long as the president had not lifted the blockade at a given port, Welles's ships would attempt to halt any merchant vessel trying to enter that port. Explicitly identifying Dix in his diary, Welles accused the general of "pressing corrupt schemes" for the benefit of the "rotten officers on his staff" and the gang of scoundrels who surrounded him.[5]

Meanwhile, Dix tried to increase the trade volumes allowable under the permit system by replacing the "military necessity" constraint with more-liberal restrictions to amounts "essential to the maintenance of our authority." Evidently sensing political liability, Stanton washed his hands of the matter by refusing to sanction any more permits, thereby motivating Dix to approach General in Chief Henry Halleck. In an effort to retain his trading monopoly, Dix began by complaining that a garrison commander in Washington, DC, had issued unauthorized permits for cargoes into and out of Norfolk, thereby implying that he wanted the practice stopped. Essentially, the general was trying to monopolize Norfolk trading permits. The Washington garrison commander was an earlier political rival to Dix.

Before Dix could make much progress, Admiral Lee told him that Secretary Welles had sent a directive requiring Lee to stop any vessel, whether with or without a permit. Dix decided to defy Lee and issued more permits. Welles felt compelled to raise the matter at a cabinet meeting with the president. Welles opined that if trade were to be initiated at Norfolk, it should be done by officially lifting the blockade. Chase advocated a permitting scheme similar to the one in use before Admiral Lee took charge. Lincoln instructed Seward and Chase to work together to formulate a policy. That night, Welles commented in his diary that Chase was generally "severe toward the Rebels except in certain matters of trade and Treasury patronage."[6]

The matter was brought up at another cabinet meeting where Stanton threw his weight behind Dix. Although no decision was made, Stanton erroneously wrote Dix that he could freely issue permits. Another cabinet meeting on October 24, 1862, was indecisive until Seward urged that the matter be delayed until after the elections in early November. Simultaneously, Great Britain's textile industries were running low on feedstock. Consequently, the country's diplomats were lobbying Seward for action to increase the supply of cotton. On November 5, 1862, the Republicans learned they lost important elections in New York and evidently decided that Dix could help mend political fences. Therefore, Lincoln directed that commerce at Norfolk be operated under the authority of the Treasury, which Chase had already put under the de facto control of Stanton and Dix. Thus, Lincoln's decision overruled the Welles viewpoint and restored an uncontested permitting system of trade at Norfolk, which was Dix's objective.[7]

Soon the number of authorized trade permits at Norfolk doubled, and redoubled. One observer estimated that eight million pounds of bacon entered the Confederacy by this route in winter 1862–1863. A month before the battle of Chancellorsville in May 1863, the meat ration of General Lee's soldiers was reduced to four ounces per day. Lieutenant General James Longstreet's entire corps was relocated to southeastern Virginia in order to gain access to more food supplies, which is why the corps was unavailable for the battle. There was deep concern that even more of Lee's army might have to be repositioned owing to the shortage. Fortunately for the Confederates, supplies allowed through Dix's trading monopoly prevented a further reduction in the size of General Lee's main force on the eve of its greatest victory.[8]

Navy Secretary Welles persistently believed that the Dix-Chase trade policies were thinly disguised methods for lining the pockets of politically well-connected businessmen. Since blockading Norfolk on a permit-exception basis was a violation of the 1856 Paris declaration upon which Lincoln justified the blockade, it must be concluded that the president demonstrated he would not consistently apply the declaration's principles when they failed to conform to his objectives.[9]

### Major General Benjamin Butler

By summer 1863, Lincoln was dissatisfied with Dix militarily, especially for failing to advance on Richmond as Lee's army was invading Pennsylvania in a campaign that culminated at Gettysburg. Dix was sent to New York, where he was in his element among the businessmen, shippers, and financiers. A few months later, in November 1863, General Benjamin Butler, who had been the maestro of interbelligerent trade earlier in New Orleans, took over at Norfolk.[10] Wherever Butler was in command, intersectional trade flourished. The general remained the district commander for fourteen months, until January 1865, which was three months before Lee's surrender at Appomattox. Historian Ludwell Johnson concluded:

> From the evidence available, there can be no doubt that a very extensive trade with the Confederacy was carried on in [Butler's Norfolk] Department. . . . This trade was extremely profitable for Northern merchants . . . and was a significant help to the Confederacy. . . . It was conducted with Butler's help and a considerable part of it was in the hands of his relatives and supporters.[11]

Shortly after arriving in Norfolk, Butler became surrounded by such men, including a number who had been with him in New Orleans. Foremost among them was Brigadier General George Shepley, who had been military governor of Louisiana. Butler invited Shepley to join him and "take care of Norfolk." After his arrival, Shepley was empowered to issue military permits allowing goods to be transported through the lines. He designated subordinate George Johnston to manage the task. In fall 1864, Johnston was charged with corruption. However, instead of being prosecuted, he was allowed to resign after saying he could show "that General Butler was a partner in all [the controversial] transactions," along with the general's brother-in-law Fisher Hildreth. Shortly thereafter, Johnston managed a thriving between-the-lines trade depot in eastern North Carolina.[12]

There is no doubt that Butler was aware of Shepley's trading activities. His own chief of staff complained about them and spoke of businessmen who "owned" Shepley. Butler took no action. Evidently, family ties were even stronger, because Hildreth seemed to be closest to the general. Hildreth had been associated with the general's older brother Andrew when Andrew was prominent in the New Orleans trade. In Norfolk, Hildreth peddled his influence with Butler for a preferential few. For example, a Baltimore merchant seeking permission to open a trade store in the area was led to believe the matter would proceed smoothly if Hildreth were provided a share of the store's ownership. Consequently, Hildreth was given a 50 percent stake although he invested no money. Similarly, he intervened for the release of an incarcerated merchant under terms requiring that upon liberation, the man open a new between-the-lines store with Hildreth and another associate as dominant shareholders.[13]

As during the Dix era, much of Butler-managed Norfolk trade was via the Dismal Swamp Canal to six northeastern counties in North Carolina separated from the rest of the state by Albemarle Sound and the Chowan River. The counties were unoccupied by either army. Northerners holding permits established stores and depots in the region. Although cotton was not a major crop, area farmers purchased bales from the Confederate government and took them through the lines to the stores, where they would be traded for "family supplies." Generally, the Southerners returned with salt, sugar, cash, and miscellaneous supplies. They used the salt to preserve butchered pork, which they sold to the Confederate commissary. After Atlantic-blockaded ports such as Charleston and Wilmington were captured, this route supplied about ten thousand pounds of bacon, sugar, coffee, and codfish daily to Lee's army. Ironically, Grant was trying to cut off Lee's supplies from the Confederacy when Lee's provender was almost entirely furnished from Yankee sources.[14]

Meanwhile, General Butler hungered for military glory and realized by late 1864 that he might never get a chance unless he acted quickly. Thus, when the opportunity came up to lead an expedition to capture Fort Fisher and thereby close the most important remaining port for blockade-runners, he jumped at the chance. His attempt, made over Christmas week 1864, was a miserable failure. Grant relieved him of command early the following month. Grant also wrote, "Whilst the army was holding Lee in Richmond and Petersburg, I found . . . [Lee] . . . was receiving supplies, either through the inefficiency or permission of [an] officer selected by General Butler . . . from Norfolk through the Albemarle and Chesapeake Canal."[15]

Butler's replacement, Major General George H. Gordon, first served several months as a subordinate when he observed:

> The control of the entire [Norfolk] region . . . was exercised by Butler. He made the laws and administered them, dealt out justice and inflicted punishment, levied fines and collected taxes. An enormous fund said [to approximate] $250,000 was created, of which Butler disposed of as he pleased. Under the permissive power of martial law he managed every movement of every person in his department.[16]

Upon assuming command, Gordon was appalled at the evidence swiftly discovered disclosing how trade at Norfolk aided the Confederacy. Reports were circulating that $100,000 of goods daily left Norfolk for Rebel armies. Grant instructed Gordon to investigate the prior trading practices at Norfolk. The result was a sixty-page indictment of Butler and his cohorts. It concluded that Butler associates, such as Hildreth and Shepley, were responsible for supplies from Butler's district pouring "directly into the departments of the Rebel Commissary and Quartermaster." Some Butler associates sold permits for a fee. One example of such a fee was fourteen cents a pound for cotton loads. Thus, a shipper bringing in ten bales from the Confederacy was required to pay a Butler crony seven hundred dollars (14 cents x 500 pounds/bale) merely for the privilege of transporting the load across Union military lines. Nonetheless, the Butler ring suffered only modest penalties, as only a few associates were caught and only temporarily imprisoned.[17]

After Lincoln's assassination, most of his political adversaries nearly silenced their criticism of the martyred president. Similarly, Gordon's report received little publicity owing to the end of the war and discoveries that reflected unfavorably on Lincoln's policies.

*Eight*

# Kirby Smithdom

AFTER THE FALL OF VICKSBURG AND PORT HUDSON IN JULY 1863, the Trans-Mississippi expanse of Texas, Arkansas, and most of Louisiana lay isolated from the rest of the Confederacy. It was almost impossible for Rebel armies to cross the river owing to patrolling Union gunboats. Soon it also became evident that Jefferson Davis and the Richmond government couldn't readily enforce laws and policies west of the river. Pragmatically, much of the governmental responsibility and authority fell to the region's overall military commander, Lieutenant General Edmund Kirby Smith. Reflecting his near dictatorial powers, residents soon assigned the region a second name: Kirby Smithdom. One Northern cotton trader explained, "Kirby Smith has full control there [Trans-Mississippi] and he cares no more about Jefferson Davis than we do."[1]

When assigned command of the Trans-Mississippi, Kirby Smith was a thirty-nine-year-old former West Point graduate from Florida. Before the Civil War, he fought in the Mexican-American War, served with the US Cavalry in Texas, and taught mathematics at West Point. After fighting in Virginia at the First Battle of Bull Run, he was given an army in eastern Tennessee. At Bull Run, he addressed his troops: "The watch word is Sumter, the signal is this," he said, throwing his right hand to his forehead with the palm outward.[2] Nobody knew what he meant, but it looked and sounded impressive. In late summer 1862, he co-operated with Lieutenant General Braxton Bragg's army on an invasion of Kentucky that was ultimately turned back at the battle of Perryville in October.

General Kirby Smith. (*Library of Congress*)

Kirby Smith became a member of Lieutenant General Leonidas Polk's anti-Bragg cabal that perpetually plagued the Rebel Army of Tennessee. He complained to President Davis that he could not readily serve under Bragg. Meanwhile, Confederate governors west of the Mississippi concluded that the aged regional commander, Lieutenant General Theophilus Holmes, was not competent for his vast territorial command. As a result, Davis gave the job to Kirby Smith in January 1863, and Holmes was demoted to head the military district of Arkansas.

Shortly after accepting Vicksburg's surrender, Union General Grant recommended to Washington that he and the Port Hudson victor, General Banks, join forces in a campaign against Mobile. A glance at a map of the United States illuminates his reasoning. It appears likely that such a move would be the fastest way to sever the Confederacy a second time and ultimately defeat it. Essentially, Grant assumed Trans-Mississippi Rebels had become inconsequential in the larger scheme of the war and could be held in check by the existing Union forces west of the river. Undoubtedly the region did not merit a major new federal offensive.[3]

However, as a military man, Grant overlooked two factors that influenced Washington and almost surely lengthened the war. First, diplomatic developments suggested that the weakened Trans-Mississippi might also be coveted by a European power. Second, the area was a tantalizing source of cotton riches. Since the two factors are linked, it is necessary to examine both. Although French intervention in Mexico was summarized earlier, the episode warrants further analysis in order to understand how it prolonged the Civil War and indirectly prompted a feeding frenzy of between-the-lines trading in Kirby Smithdom.

## French Ambitions

Louis-Napoleon Bonaparte was elected president of the Second French Republic in 1848 at age thirty-nine. While less famous than his uncle, he was nonetheless a monarchist with grand ambitions. Thus, within four years he became a dictator, Emperor Napoleon III of the Second French Empire. Owing to fiscal mismanagement and other difficulties, his government was forced to become less authoritarian by the time of the American Civil War. Nonetheless, the emperor remained hungry to reestablish French glory. Our Civil War and a simultaneous Mexican fiscal crisis offered an opportunity to colonize part—perhaps a big part—of the American continent.

France lost its last major stake in the Western Hemisphere when it sold New Orleans and the Louisiana Territory in 1803. Since then, the United States had absorbed half of Mexico, first by the annexation of Texas and then by the Mexican Cession comprising the state of California and much of the lands east of it to Texas following the end of the Mexican-American War. Louis-Napoleon reasoned that Lincoln would be too focused on suppressing the Southern rebellion to oppose an armed French presence in Mexico, which could provide a base from which he could help the Confederacy win independence. If successful, the Monroe Doctrine would become impotent, and the Western Hemisphere might once again become fertile territory of European colonies.[4]

To review, in summer 1861, Mexico suspended payments on $62 million in debt principally held by Europeans. Consequently, that December, Britain, Spain, and France seized the port at Veracruz, where they collected import-export duties and applied the funds to debt repayments. When a French expeditionary force arrived in March 1862, Spain and Britain left because they sensed that France might seek to form a vassal state in Mexico rather than merely collect debts for European creditors. Initially the French met temporary defeat, but by summer 1863, they had captured Mexico City with an army of forty thousand, forcing President Benito Juarez to flee. He first went to San Luis Potosi and later to Chihuahua on the remote border with Texas.

For most of the nineteenth century, the reigning monarch of Europe's Hapsburg family was Franz Joseph (he was emperor of Austria-Hungary from 1848 until his death during World War I). Only two years younger, his brother Ferdinand Maximilian was left without a meaningful office when he matured into adulthood. Nonetheless, other European monarchs and the pope recognized his royalty. That was important to supportive Mexican factions, such as clerics of the Roman Catholic Church and political conservatives who longed for the steady hand of a monarch after dozens of temporary governments following Mexican independence only forty years earlier. After a French army occupied Mexico City, the conquering general nominated a list of thirty-five notables who appointed a three-man regency to rule the country until a monarchy could be established. The regency consisted of two Mexican generals and the archbishop of Mexico.[5] The group promptly voted to invite Maximilian to become emperor of Mexico. It sent a delegation to his Miramar castle in Trieste (in present-day Italy) to present the offer personally.[6]

On October 3, 1863, Archduke Maximilian accepted on condition that he be approved by a "vote of the whole country," which he may not have realized was a foregone conclusion under the glittering bayonets of the occupying French army.[7]

> Maximilian's response propelled French columns into the countryside seeking signatures on petitions, which begged the Archduke to rule over Mexico. The soldiers went to . . . all the chief cities in Mexico, and they destroyed anyone who stood in their way. . . . A column would appear outside a town and, if there were any opposition, throw a few shells into it, accept its surrender and be hailed as the liberators of the country. Lines of men and women would offer thanks for the coming of the French. Then their signatures . . . would be affixed to the petitions addressed to Maximilian.[8]

Maximilian I, left, of Mexico. He was the younger brother of Austrian emperor Franz Joseph. Napoleon III, right, emperor of France. (*Library of Congress*)

It was evident to everyone except perhaps the archduke and his wife that he would have no power without the presence of the French army. Soon it was apparent he was a puppet monarch of Napoleon III's.

Maximilian did not arrive in Mexico City until June 1864. Prior to that he consulted with many dignitaries to formulate and communicate his policies. One of the first was a Mr. de Haviland, an acquaintance of Jefferson Davis's from Washington who was visiting Trieste on mysterious business. In a letter to John Slidell, who was the Confederate minister to Paris, de Haviland wrote in November 1863: "Maximilian expressed the warmest possible interest in the Confederate cause. He said he considered it identical with that of the new Mexican Empire . . . that he was particularly desirous that his sentiments upon this subject should be known to the Confederate President."[9]

Since Maximilian did not propose to adopt slavery, it is likely that the "identical" cause was that of independence and free trade. (Lincoln's government had adopted import tariffs of nearly 50 percent to finance the war and promote the interests of Northern industrialists and their ecosystem.)

After reading the letter, Slidell visited the Mexican mission in Paris, where he was told de Haviland's remarks were valid. At the

Foreign Office, he was informed that Maximilian "attached the greatest importance" to official diplomatic recognition of the Confederacy by European governments. Confederate propagandist James Wilson met several times with Maximilian, who spoke of desiring that France recognize the Confederacy before he was crowned in Mexico City.[10]

But it was not to be. Before embarking for Mexico, Maximilian visited Louis-Napoleon in Paris in March 1864, and the two concluded it was not a good idea to recognize the Confederacy before the Civil War was settled. Immediate recognition ran the risk of war with the United States, whereas a hypothetical future Southern victory would permit Mexico to recognize the Confederacy without provoking a fight with the United States. While temporarily visiting Paris, the French minister to Washington told Slidell that Lincoln was overheard to say "[Maximilian's] government would be recognized in Washington if the Mexican monarchy declined to recognize the Confederacy."[11] That did not happen either, although the rumor was also reported in the *London Globe* newspaper about the same time.[12]

More alarming to Washington were reports that Napoleon III was interested in Texas. Such rumors had circulated among Lincoln's informers for almost a year. In January 1863, an Austrian diplomat claimed Confederates were dismayed to learn that French consuls in Galveston and Richmond suggested to Texans that they should withdraw from the Davis government. In July, Secretary of State Seward told other cabinet members, "Louis-Napoleon is making an effort to get Texas." In September, a Vienna newspaper presumptively reported, "The French government is supposed to have arranged with the Southern American states for the cession of Texas."[13]

Less than a month after the fall of Vicksburg in July 1863, Lincoln asked Secretary of War Stanton, "Can we not renew the effort to organize a force to go to west Texas? . . . I believe no local object is now more important."[14] It had been only fifteen years since the end of the Mexican-American War. If the Mexican vassal government could be made to covet the return of Texas, there were worries that it might also seek to reacquire the state of California or territories included in the present states of Arizona, Nevada, and New Mexico.[15] Some rumors even suggested that the French would seek to annex Louisiana as well.[16]

Confederate War Department clerk John B. Jones also learned of the Texas and Louisiana rumors in January 1863. He believed them to be genuine. "The Emperor of France is charged with a design to seize Mexico . . . and to recognize Texas separately, making [it] a dependency from which cotton may be [supplied]. [It is said] the French . . . are endeavoring to detach Texas from the Confederacy. . . . I have no doubt of its genuineness. . . . If Texas leaves us so may Louisiana."[17]

Consequently, in January 1864, California senator James McDougall proposed a congressional resolution stating that French intervention in Mexico was "an act unfriendly to the republic of the United States." It called on the French to withdraw by March 15 and threatened war if they didn't. After the resolution was tabled in February, McDougall softened the language to read, "the occupation of Mexico . . . by the Emperor of France . . . or by . . . [the] Emperor of Mexico, is an offense to the people of the republic of the United States." On March 23, Seward sent a copy of the less bellicose decree to the US mission in Paris while Maximilian was visiting the city. The following month, the US House unanimously approved a resolution stating, "The Congress of the United States are unwilling . . . to leave . . . the impression that they are indifferent . . . [to] the deplorable events . . . in Mexico and . . . declare that it does not . . . acknowledge any monarchial government erected on the ruins of any republican government in America under the auspices of any European power."[18]

Although Massachusetts senator Sumner blocked the resolution from the Senate floor, Seward also sent a copy to the US legation in Paris with a note expressing the informed opinion that it reflected the sentiments of the Northern people. At Lincoln's nomination for a second term in June, the Baltimore convention adopted a declaration stating, "The people of the United States can never regard with indifference the attempt of any European power to overthrow . . .

the institutions of any republican government on the Western continent and . . . they shall view as menacing to the peace . . . any efforts . . . to obtain new footholds for monarchial governments . . . in close proximity to the United States." Although Lincoln's public statements softened the party's position, he told Major General John M. Thayer he wanted to fight only one war at a time and would address Mexico after the Confederacy was defeated. He added presciently, "When the [French] army is gone, the Mexicans will take care of Maximilian."[19]

Not knowing that Louis-Napoleon and Maximilian had agreed during their March 1864 Paris meeting that the Mexican monarch should decline to recognize the Confederacy, Davis was eager to establish an alliance because of the archduke's earlier, more favorable remarks. In January 1864, he designated the former US minister to Spain, William Preston, as envoy to the Mexican court even though Maximilian would not arrive for five months. Preston first went to Havana, from which he could more quickly reach Mexico City when the new emperor arrived. But he grew impatient and went to London and Paris, where he gradually realized that an alliance was unlikely.[20]

After the June 1863 French occupation of Mexico City, Lincoln followed up on his comments that a federal military presence should be established in Texas with August 1863 letters to Generals Banks and Grant. To Banks in New Orleans he wrote, "recent events in Mexico render early action in Texas more important than ever." His letter to Grant said, "in view of recent events in Mexico I am greatly impressed with the importance of reestablishing national authority in Western Texas as soon as possible." The letters would lead to three military operations that historians generally conclude prolonged the war. For example, Bruce Catton claimed that the movements against Texas were "a substantial error" and "a move in the wrong direction."[21]

If Grant and Banks had advanced against Mobile in August or September, Confederate General Polk and his fifteen thousand soldiers would have been unable to reinforce General Bragg to help win the battle of Chickamauga in late September 1863. Moreover, the reinforcements actually received by Bragg from Lee's Virginia army might have been split between Bragg and Polk. If so, Bragg would have lost his numerical advantage against Union General Rosecrans at Chickamauga and may thereby have failed to win a victory that delayed the Union offensive against Atlanta by six months.

The first move prompted by Lincoln's wish to occupy part of Texas was a September 8, 1863, attack on Sabine Pass on the coastline at the Louisiana-Texas border. General Banks sent an amphibious force, including five thousand infantry, to the pass. It was the starting point of a clever plan to seize the railroad at Beaumont and make a quick descent on Houston and Galveston before any Rebel army could respond. The only opposition was a small fort at Sabine Pass manned by fewer than fifty soldiers who were former Irish dockworkers. But without the loss of a single soldier, the Rebels, under twenty-five-year-old Lieutenant Richard Dowling, surprisingly repulsed the federal attack.[22]

In November 1863, Banks dispatched another amphibious force, including six thousand infantry under Major General Napoleon Dana, to capture Brownsville in an effort to put an end to the Matamoros trade. He seized the town, thereby forcing caravans to and from Matamoros to cross the Rio Grande hundreds of miles farther upstream at Laredo or Eagle Pass. After securing Brownsville, Dana moved up the Texas coast, capturing towns such as Corpus Christi and the railheads at Indianola and Port Lavaca. Owing to a sectional dispute dating to the Mexican-American War, the federals occupying Brownsville discovered they had an ally in Mexican warlord Juan Cortina, who temporarily controlled Matamoros. Nonetheless, even though Cortina was hostile to Confederates, he permitted trade to continue, albeit with higher tariffs.

Shortly after occupying Brownsville, Union officers tried to convince Matamoros officials to confiscate Confederate cotton for the benefit of the United States. While negotiations were in progress, an officer named Herbert, who was connected with the Lincoln-selected military governor of Texas, concluded a potentially lucrative private trade deal for himself with the governor of the Mexican state in which Matamoros was located. Although Herbert was court-martialed, Washington authorities released him on a technicality.[23]

Banks's west Texas offensive appeared to be progressing toward an eventual Rebel capitulation of Galveston, but it was interrupted by orders from Washington. General in Chief Halleck wanted Banks to ascend Louisiana's Red River to capture Kirby Smith's headquarters at Shreveport and move into Texas from the east. Halleck ordered that the west Texas federals abandon their offensive. Except for a small force to hold Brownsville, he directed the rest to return to New Orleans to join Banks for a more powerful push up the Red River. Ultimately Halleck's order would lead to a frenzy of corrupted cotton trade.[24]

While Banks was launching his Red River campaign in March 1864, the soldiers remaining at Brownsville under Major General Francis Herron moved up the Rio Grande to further disrupt Matamoros trade. They temporarily occupied Laredo but were driven out by Confederate partisans who were mostly of Mexican ancestry under the leadership of Colonel Santos Benavides. In July 1864, regular Confederate cavalry under Colonel "Rip" Ford recaptured Brownsville, thereby once again enabling the town to become a thriving import-export center. Herron's federals withdrew to Brazos Island, where they held an insignificant stretch of Texas beach until the end of the war. The Yankee-allied Mexican warlord Cortina was driven out of Matamoros by the French army in September 1864, as Confederate troops helped the Frenchmen by taking a few potshots across the Rio Grande at Cortina's men.[25]

## Red River Cotton

Although the Red River campaign in spring 1864 was represented as an offensive to free Louisiana and Arkansas of Rebel armies and plant the US flag in Texas as a warning to Louis-Napoleon and Maximilian, there were additional motivations. One was a Northern craving for cotton. A second was to buttress political support for Lincoln. The president wanted to establish loyal governments in Louisiana and Arkansas so that the two states could send Lincoln supporters to the 1864 presidential nominating convention set for Baltimore in June and provide Lincoln-faithful voters for the general election later in the year.[26]

Late in 1863, more than one hundred five thousand bales of cotton owned by the Confederate Treasury were crowding the wharves of the Ouachita and Red rivers in the District of Western Louisiana. Given that the average New York price of upland middling cotton was over one dollar a pound in 1864, such inventories were worth over $50 million, which translates to almost $800 million in inflation-adjusted 2013 dollars.[27] (The price of cotton actually rose to a high of $1.90 a pound in 1864.)[28] And there was considerably more cotton in the same district owned by private growers and their merchants.[29] A 10 percent tax-in-kind authorized in Richmond fell due on March 1, 1864, that would give the Confederate government title to one-tenth of the Trans-Mississippi's 1863 cotton crop. Such cotton could be legally confiscated.[30]

Origins of the Red River campaign date to 1861, when mill owner Edward Atkinson distributed his pamphlet proposing to transform Southern agriculture by settling a portion of Texas with free Northern white laborers. He predicted his system would produce three times as much cotton and would eventually force the South to abandon slavery.[31] General Butler joined in the chorus but, as discussed, was first given the opportunity to become rich by trading with the enemy in New Orleans. In October 1862, the *New York Times* editorialized, "Texas alone is capable . . . of producing more cotton annually than all the South ever exported by the aid of its four million slaves."[32] Once Mississippi River navigation was cleared with the capture of Vicksburg, a combination of diplomatic, political, and mercenary factors converged to give birth to the Red River campaign, as planning began in January 1864.

Interest in upper Louisiana cotton and an expedition up the Red River was reignited that month by the arrival of three thousand bales in New Orleans from upriver Natchez, Mississippi. Michael Hahn, who would soon be elected governor of a Lincoln-loyal Lousiana state government, wrote the president that the arrival from Natchez "produced such a sensation as to cause a large number of persons to take the oath of allegiance in order to resume their business." Within a few months, a US marshal in Louisiana wrote Lincoln, "Commerce is still King. You have it in your power to reduce the price of gold, pacify the clamor for cotton from abroad, make friends for yourself and country and put into the exchequer from this department some $30–$40 million."[33]

On January 23, 1864, General Banks replied to a letter from General in Chief Halleck that Banks had completely accepted Halleck's views regarding the merits of an advance up the Red River. Earlier that month, Banks learned that two Confederate officers were willing to be bribed in order to ensure that massive quantities of cotton were not burned ahead of an advancing Union army, as otherwise required by Confederate law. Banks was an ambitious politician with eyes on the White House. He knew that if he could deliver sizable quantities of cotton to New England, powerful politicians would be influenced to look favorably on a Banks candidacy.[34]

Since he was disconnected from Richmond after the fall of Vicksburg, Kirby Smith organized a Trans-Mississippi Cotton Bureau in August 1863, at his Shreveport headquarters. Formation of the bureau was tantamount to the presumption of military control over a major sector of the civilian economy in a manner that was not practiced east of the Mississippi. It was the first important step toward "Kirby Smithdom," the informal label applied to the nearly dictatorial domain in which Smith assumed sweeping powers over nearly all military and many civilian aspects of life in the Trans-Mississippi. As described by author Robert Kerby:

> After the first few hesitant months, there was nothing very subtle about the way [intersectional commerce] was conducted. Whenever a river steamboat churned from Shreveport or Alexandria, Louisiana, with a cargo of cotton consigned to New Orleans it was fairly obvious that responsible people were permitting trade across the lines. Rebel customs officials collected the duties due on smuggled shipments of contraband, while New York financiers openly dealt in shares of Confederate cotton. Swarms of Northern cotton buyers, bearing licenses signed by

> Lincoln himself, endured the rude hospitality of Shreveport, while agents dispatched by Kirby Smith . . . became accustomed to the amenities of New Orleans and Washington. The trade even reunited families rent apart by passions of the war.[35]

Since much Trans-Mississippi trade earlier in the war was across the Rio Grande, in 1862 the Confederate War Department designated a single man as the region's exclusive purchasing agent. He was Major Simeon Hart of San Antonio, who had excellent connections in Mexico and Richmond. Hart was expected to become the prime supplier of munitions and supplies for Trans-Mississippi armies.

However, he was hindered by an inability to pay market prices for cotton, which was the only "international currency" native to the territory. Soon his suppliers—overseas and in the North—were demanding cotton for items previously delivered and unpaid for, as well as for future shipments. Trans-Mississippi Rebel armies badly needed supplies. In summer 1863, one-third of Arkansas enlisted men were without arms. A few months later, Kirby Smith estimated that ten thousand soldiers in his entire command were unarmed. In spring 1864, he complained that "one large battle . . . would leave us without powder and but little lead."[36]

By May 1863, Hart had concluded that the only way he could get the required cotton was to impress it, by force if necessary. He wrote Confederate Major General James Magruder, commanding in Texas, for permission to impress cotton. When Magruder did not respond, he wrote Richmond, where his request got tangled up in red tape, although President Davis eventually replied inconclusively that he "never intended to employ such means except as a last resort."[37] By then, however, events in the Trans-Mississippi had already settled the matter.

On May 20, 1863, a British steamer carrying a large load of Enfield rifles for Major Hart arrived off the mouth of the Rio Grande. The skipper demanded prompt payment of two thousand cotton bales before he would release the cargo. Hart again wrote Magruder for an order empowering him to impress cotton.

Magruder forwarded the letter to Kirby Smith in Shreveport. Kirby Smith tried to get Magruder to write the order, but when the latter refused, Smith finally yielded on June 27, 1863, and took responsibility for authorizing impressment. He even went further and authorized impressment of wagons and transportation equipment when required. Magruder acted quickly, and by August 1863, there was hardly a bale of privately owned cotton in Texas south of the Nueces River, which was the Brownsville district.

Texas growers were furious because the export market provided much better prices than those designated on the Confederate impressment schedule. Moreover, the export market could pay in specie, whereas impressment was made with Confederate financial instruments. It was partly to address such complaints that Kirby Smith organized the Cotton Bureau under the leadership of Lieutenant Colonel William A. Broadwell. Owing to the size of Texas and its large volumes of cotton, Broadwell opened a branch of the bureau in Houston. Although officially a jurisdictional branch of Shreveport, the Houston office acted independently. It announced that Texas growers were required to sell half their crop to the bureau at fixed prices while the other half could be sold on the free market. However, growers were required to provide transportation of all the cargo, including the portion impressed by the army.

The order triggered two unintended consequences. First, many growers rushed to sell available inventories at bargain prices to buyers on the free market. Second, Governor Pendleton Murrah and the Texas legislature responded with a plan to provide planters a legal alternative offering better prices than Cotton Bureau impressment. They organized the Texas State Military Board, which was authorized to supply ordnance and supplies for Texas militia. The board was approved to issue $2 million worth of bonds backed by Texas land, as opposed to depreciated currency. Such bonds could be used to buy cotton because the growers would accept them owing to the real estate backing the securities.

Murrah implemented a policy whereby cotton would be purchased with the bonds and transported across the Rio Grande.

Once it was in Mexico, the Texas board would return title to half of the cotton to the original owner. Since all of the cotton was officially "owned" by the state of Texas while in transit, the Confederate Cotton Bureau could not seize it because government-owned cotton was exempt from Confederate impressment. By March 1864, about one hundred thousand bales had already been sold to the state.

In Shreveport, Cotton Bureau leader Broadwell responded by imploring Kirby Smith to impress whatever cotton was needed, even if it was "officially" owned by the state of Texas. The general felt compelled to react with dictatorial regulations. Every cotton grower was required to sell half of his volume to the Cotton Bureau. Only those traders licensed by the bureau could engage in international commerce. Essentially, the general nationalized cotton trade, nearly transforming it into a Confederate government monopoly.

Murrah protested the latest moves by the Cotton Bureau as a usurpation of states' rights. Kirby Smith responded that the conflicting Texas regulations eviscerated the Confederacy's ability to defend itself west of the Mississippi River. Even some Texas newspapers supported the general. Murrah and Kirby Smith met personally in July 1864, after which the governor capitulated. He concluded that the survival of the army and Texas itself required unencumbered importation of military supplies, which the army could not purchase without cotton. Nonetheless, impressment remained unpopular and was sometimes abused by imposters. For example, in May 1864, three bogus "impressment officers" were hanged in Lavaca County, Texas, after seizing property and threatening the lives of unwilling victims.

Although President Davis later restrained some of the harshest Cotton Bureau regulations, the pragmatic effects were minimal. The bureau functioned and prospered until February 1865, when its duties were assumed by the Confederate Treasury Agency in Marshall, Texas.[38] Interbelligerent cotton trade in the Trans-Mississippi after the fall of Vicksburg not only enabled Confederates to keep an army in the field but also provided them enough support to turn back two federal offensives and launch an invasion of Missouri during the 1864 presidential elections.[39]

Although planning started in January, the federal Red River offensive did not get under way until March 10, 1864. Components of three Union armies and one navy flotilla started to converge on Kirby Smith's headquarters at Shreveport. General Banks, with twenty thousand troops, would first combine forces with Admiral Porter and General A. J. Smith with ten thousand soldiers at Alexandria to advance on Shreveport from the southeast. However, Smith's troops were only temporarily loaned from Sherman's army and were supposed to start returning to Sherman by April 15. Union General Frederick Steele was to advance with twelve thousand men from Little Rock and Fort Smith, Arkansas, thereby approaching Shreveport from the northeast.

While Smith and Porter were instructed to "cooperate" with Banks, the Massachusetts general lacked direct authority over them. The force proceeding to Shreveport from the southeast included a total of thirty thousand effectives of all arms, with ninety cannon and Porter's flotilla of thirteen ironclads and nine other vessels. The movement from Arkansas was delayed partly because Union troops were needed to supervise voter ratification of a Union-loyal state constitution and election of a federally recognized governor. Lincoln desired the election so that the state might provide delegates to the June presidential nominating convention. The presence of federal troops nearly assured a favorable vote. The new Arkansas constitution was ratified on March 14, 1864, and Isaac Murphy was inaugurated governor the following month.[40] Because of obligations to supervise the election and his own reluctance for the expedition, Steele did not get started until March 25.[41] Although he was also directed to "cooperate" with Banks, he would be mostly on his own until the two Union pincers could connect, presumably somewhere in northern Louisiana during April.[42]

Kirby Smith had been expecting such an enemy offensive for months and was easily persuaded to quickly sell cotton to most any buyer rather than be forced to burn it ahead of a federal advance. Between Louisiana and Arkansas he had at most twelve thousand

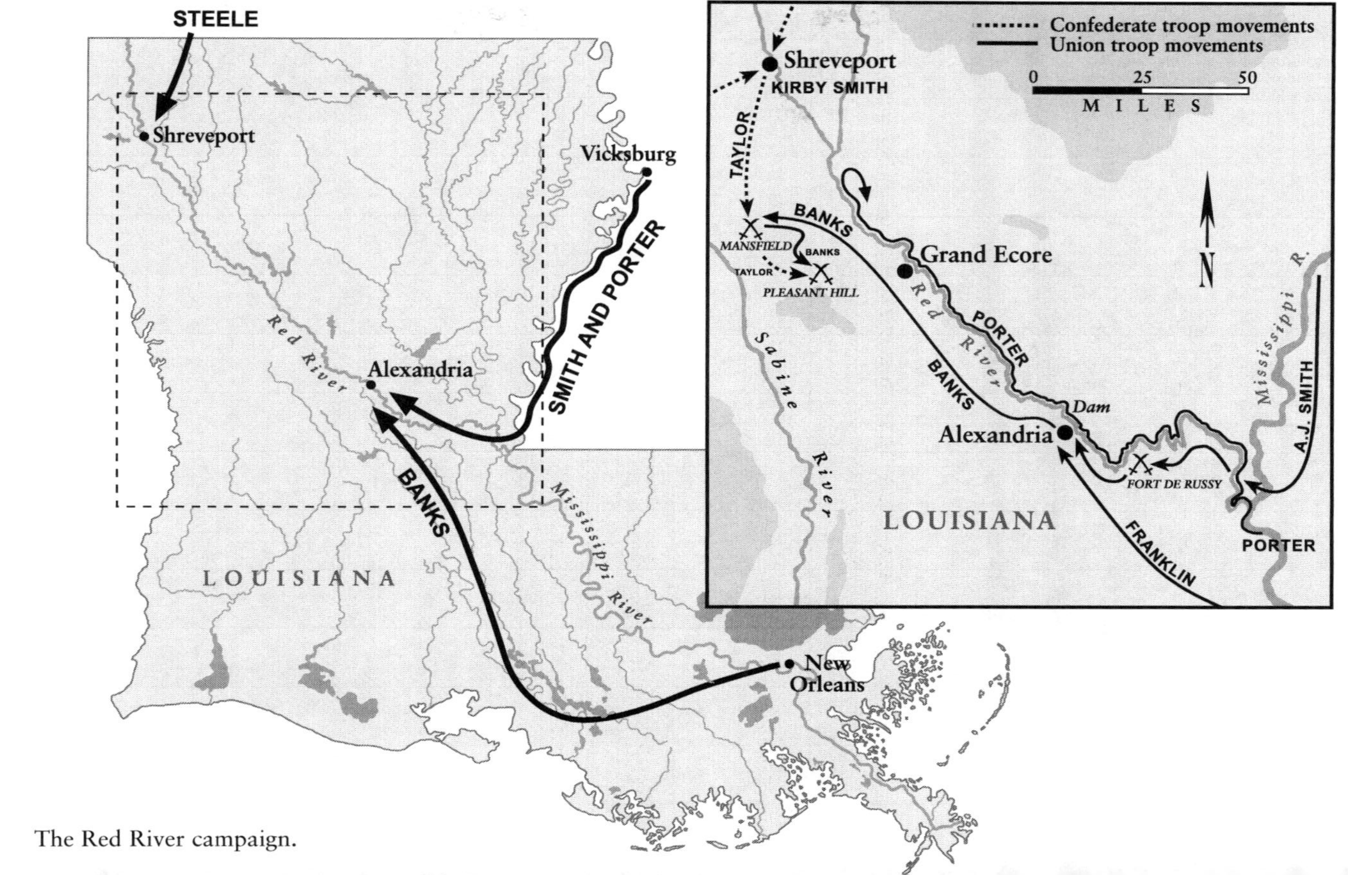


The Red River campaign.

troops to resist a combined forty-two thousand Union soldiers plus Admiral Dixon's flotilla. While he could call on additional troops from distant points in Texas, few could be expected to arrive rapidly. Thus, it was improbable that his command could climb to as high as twenty thousand men during the present emergency. Given the numbers and resources of the opposing federals, a sizable loss of cotton inventories was a near certainty, whether they were sold, confiscated, or burned.

Prior to the military advance on the Red River, cotton traders and well-connected individuals approached President Lincoln, General Banks, and others with various schemes to get cotton inventories out of the region before Confederates burned them. By February, Banks estimated a combination of proposals could secure as much as two hundred thousand to three hundred thousand bales, which would equal $100 million to $150 million, at an average price of one dollar per pound, to the final textile industry buyers. Given the large sums involved, it's not surprising that nearly all the proposals were self-serving to those originating them, including many who were untrustworthy.[43]

One example was a secret Confederate sympathizer and director of the Union-loyal Louisiana State Bank, John Stevenson. On behalf of the bank, he held title to about twenty thousand bales behind Confederate lines in northern Louisiana. He wished to ship them to George Arnold & Company in Liverpool, where they would be sold and the proceeds credited to the Louisiana bank. The bank would first apply such proceeds to an outstanding Stevenson loan. The balance would be credited to his account. However, he secretly agreed that the Confederacy could use his excess credit to buy munitions and supplies in Great Britain. Stevenson obtained a document authorizing the shipment, which was signed by Lincoln, Louisiana military governor Shepley, and the New Orleans customs collector.

But Stevenson's plans were frustrated by a conflicting agreement between Banks and two men named McKee. Confederate Major Andrew W. McKee, who later disappeared and may have obtained his position under false pretenses, was the ranking purchasing agent in Shreveport's Cotton Bureau. His cousin, J. H. McKee, was a civilian speculator on the Union side. The civilian McKee told Banks that his cousin could delay Confederate orders for cotton burning once the campaign was under way in exchange for payments of eighteen cents a pound on bales turned over to the federal army. Banks planned that cotton secured through the proposal would be auctioned, with proceeds paid to the US Treasury except for fees owed to the McKees. Once Banks began his march, the McKees blocked Stevenson's shipment because the banker's bales were among those the cousins wanted to reserve for Banks.[44]

Eventually, Major McKee was convicted of multiple charges in a Confederate court-martial, but he was released by a civilian court. It was later learned that the Confederate War Department had no record of a Major Andrew W. McKee and that he had previously arranged numerous transfers of Confederate cotton through the lines. After his release by the civilian court, he jumped bail and vanished.[45]

Ten days before Christmas Eve 1863, Lincoln signed a pass for former Kentucky congressman Samuel Casey to travel multiple times to Shreveport and be given safe passage when returning with cargo. (Casey was a brother-in-law of General Grant's.)[46] While en route, he learned that Porter's flotilla would accompany Banks up the Red River. Casey sent a telegram to Lincoln, stating, "Do not let Admiral Porter send an expedition up the Red River until you hear from me again. If he should, he will defeat all my plans." Astonishingly, he was trying to require the US military to adjust its plans to accommodate his business proposition.[47]

Casey found Shreveport to be an active commercial center. Since the occupation of Brownsville in November, Kirby Smith had determined it was more expedient to sell cotton across enemy lines than to export it to Mexico. Contrary to US Treasury regulations, Casey used British pounds instead of the US greenbacks legally required to purchase twenty thousand bales from Kirby Smith's Cotton Bureau. On returning to Washington in February, Casey learned that agents for international buyers in New Orleans were attempting to derail the transaction.

Casey hurriedly met with Lincoln again. This time he secured a signed paper naming Casey and several other men as the owners of the specified cotton and instructing the military to provide any necessary protection required for the shipment. One of the other owners mentioned in the president's note was his friend William Butler. Casey rushed back to Louisiana but only arrived in time to become one of many cotton speculators trailing in the wake of Banks's army.[48]

Shortly before arriving in Alexandria to meet General Smith's column and Admiral Dixon's flotilla, General Banks settled on a cotton policy. He would allow loyal citizens to ship their inventories to New Orleans so long as none had ever been owned by the Confederate government. Owners would be permitted to sell their bales at New Orleans. However, one-third of the proceeds would be withheld by the US Treasury until it could be determined that none of the cash was to be used in a manner damaging to the United States. All cotton owned by the Confederate government would be seized and sold at auction for the benefit of the US Treasury, except for such fees payable to persons like the McKees for helping to locate and identify it.

When Banks reached Alexandria on March 24, he was shocked to see Admiral Porter's sailors continually loading cotton onto their boats as a prize of war. It was probably the most conspicuous incidence of Porter's earning his "Thief of the Mississippi" nom de guerre. His men scoured the countryside painting "C. S. A." on any bales they found in order to falsely represent them as property of the Confederate government and therefore subject to seizure under prize law. Next they would strike a line through the "C. S. A." initials and add "U. S. N." to signify the change in ownership to the US Navy. Afterward, locals facetiously remarked that Porter's "C. S. A.–U. S. N." stenciling was an abbreviation for "Cotton Stealing Association of the United States Navy."

Porter's cotton seizures not only enraged Southern growers, they also demoralized federal soldiers. To review, maritime prize law awarded a portion of captured cargoes to the applicable naval vessel. Such goods could be sold at auction, with the proceeds divided

"Commodore Porter's fleet before Alexandria, March 26 [1864]." (*Library of Congress*)

among the crew. Not only were Porter's seizures often miles from the riverbanks and exempt as noncontraband, but federal troops were dispirited to witness sailors profiting personally under the envious eyes of infantrymen who could not participate merely because they served in a different military branch. Animosity intensified on their learning that the admiralty prize court with jurisdiction was in Porter's home base of Cairo, Illinois. Even in official correspondence, at least one army officer grumbled, "every gunboat is loaded with cotton and the officers are taking it without regard to the loyalty of the owners. It looks . . . like a big steal." [49]

Like those of other officers who seized private property, Porter's actions violated the Lieber Code issued by Lincoln on April 23, 1863, as General Order 100, "Instructions for the Government of Armies of the United States in the Field." Among others, Articles 37 and 38 were violated without consequence:

> Article 37. The United States acknowledge and protect, in hostile countries occupied by them . . . strictly private property; . . . Offenses to the contrary shall be rigorously punished.
>
> Article 38. Private property . . . can be seized only by way

> of military necessity, for the support or other benefit of the army or of the United States. If the owner has not fled, the commanding officer will cause receipts to be given, which may serve the spoliated [sic] owner to obtain indemnity.[50]

No doubt a clever lawyer like Butler would argue that Articles 37 and 38 did not apply because rebellious states like Louisiana, Texas, and Arkansas were not "hostile countries."

Presumably, General Banks was dismayed by Porter's seizure because it ruined his arrangement with the McKees to spare some cotton from the Rebel army torch. No doubt the McKees and Samuel Casey were even more bitterly disappointed. Since Admiral Porter was not his subordinate, Banks could not order him to cease or change his practices, despite the fact that the admiral had been instructed to "cooperate" with the general.[51]

As a result of military defeats, low water, and supply difficulties, Banks, Porter, and Steele were forced to abandon efforts to capture Shreveport or hoist the flag of the United States in east Texas. Banks's retreat was occasioned by additional civilian property destruction, which likely included cotton. On May 7, Union Major General Canby was assigned command of the Military Division of West Mississippi and was to direct all operations of the Departments of the Gulf and Arkansas, thereby making both Banks and Steele subordinate to him. A few days earlier, Steele had returned to Little Rock with a hungry but intact army. Banks and Porter did not reach safety until May 20, after burning Alexandria and leaving much of central Louisiana in burned-out desolation. As Confederate Major General Richard Taylor, whose army pursued Banks, remembered: "In [the army's] rapid flight from Grand Ecore to Monette's Ferry, a distance of forty miles, the Federals burned nearly every house on the road. In pursuit we passed the smoking ruins of homesteads, by which stood weeping women and children."[52]

Banks gathered a total of only about four thousand cotton bales, of which twenty-five hundred went to C. A. Weed & Company in New Orleans. Earlier, Weed had been a business partner of General

Butler's shady older brother, Andrew. The privileged cotton owned by Samuel Casey and Lincoln's friend William Butler fell victim to an unexpected military emergency. When Porter attempted to return downstream after Banks was defeated at the battle of Mansfield, he discovered that the water on the Red River had dropped so low he could not get his ships across the rapids at Alexandria. He was saved by an enterprising Wisconsin engineer who hurriedly constructed a series of dams that provided a channel deep enough for the vessels to get through. Like those of many others, Casey's cotton bales were appropriated for use as dam construction materials. As a result, Porter sent only about six thousand bales to the prize court.[53]

Porter's unrestrained confiscations at Alexandria early in the campaign are probably largely responsible for Banks's failure to return with much cotton. The admiral's methods persuaded Southerners upstream from Alexandria to burn most of their cotton. About one hundred fifty thousand bales were burned to avoid letting the Yankees get them for free.[54]

When Porter later testified before the Congressional Joint Committee on the Conduct of the War, he artfully, but falsely, characterized the entire campaign as an enterprise to obtain cotton for Banks and people connected to him. When asked about the cotton seizures under naval prize law, he simply lied: "It was seized as government cotton and sent to the courts without any application on the part of the navy as prize law at all." Nonetheless, about two months after the campaign ended, Congress passed a law stipulating that no property taken on inland waters could be considered a maritime prize. Porter is estimated to have collected over $90,000 personally before the change.[55]

The allegations of personal corruption and profiteering against Banks, who returned with little cotton and was defeated militarily, were unjust. The congressional committee needed a villain. Porter's successful military record unfairly gave him immunity and conferred a false credibility on his accusations against Banks. Those subordinates who were sensitive to the direction of the political wind merely piled on with more false or one-sided accounts.

Author Michael Thomas Smith concluded, "Whatever the hopes of merchants in New Orleans and elsewhere . . . Banks did not intend that he or anyone else in his army should make a profit from Red River cotton."[56]

Kirby Smith continued to sell cotton to sustain Confederate armies west of the Mississippi through the end of 1864. But the 1864 regional cotton crop was poor. By Christmas, his armies owed $40 million to citizens from whom goods had been purchased or impressed with vouchers. As merchants increasingly stopped accepting the vouchers, the cotton-impressment system began to collapse. In February 1865, Kirby Smith's chief quartermaster advised him, "We . . . cannot impress; have no currency; the army is in want; it cannot be supplied." The next month, Smith authorized his chief of subsistence to seize whatever supplies were required by force, regardless of whether vouchers were accepted. In one of its final actions, Congress later affirmed Smith's decision with a new act in mid-March requiring citizens from whom supplies were impressed to accept promissory notes throughout the Confederacy, and not merely the Trans-Mississippi.[57]

In January 1865, it was discovered that the general in charge of the Texas militia had embezzled every cent earned by the Texas Military Cotton Board during the preceding six months. He and an accomplice had deposited the money in a Havana bank. Before it could be recovered, the war was over. In the final months, Kirby Smith's Cotton Bureau was hopelessly in arrears. It did not have the money, or cotton, to pay for items purchased in the concluding months. The bureau and Kirby Smith were accused of fraud and corruption. The *San Antonio News* wrote that he "has been engaged in Cotton Speculation on his own account. We know that he has been trading, openly, with the enemy." The complaints reached Richmond, where President Davis appointed three prominent Westerners to investigate the matter a month before Lee's surrender at Appomattox.[58]

Nothing came of the investigation. Like Banks, Kirby Smith was more victim than villain. Outraged politicians and civilians wanted somebody to blame for the harsh living conditions in the

Trans-Mississippi during the closing months of the war. Although the cotton impressments were undeniably a hardship, there is no significant evidence that Kirby Smith personally profited from them. While the record of Major McKee alone confirms a level of corruption in the Cotton Bureau, it does not appear that Kirby Smith profited.

After the war, Smith immigrated briefly to Mexico but returned a year later to head the Atlantic & Pacific Telegraph Company. The company failed within a few years, and in 1870, Smith was named president of the University of Nashville. He left Nashville in 1875 to become a mathematics professor at the University of the South in Sewanee, Tennessee, until 1893, when he died of pneumonia. He was the last surviving Confederate lieutenant general.

Shortly after the Red River campaign, the US Congress and certain Union military leaders could no longer abide the volume and endemic corruption of intersectional trade. Congress enacted legislation intended to control it, while a number of military commanders became less accommodating of speculators—even those who had signed authorizations. Nonetheless, the potential profits remained tantalizing. Lincoln concluded he could not allow the availability of cotton to dwindle to a trickle without unacceptable economic, political, and diplomatic consequences. So he adopted policies to circumvent the congressional restrictions and opened between-the-lines trading wider than ever before.[59]

*Nine*

# Eyes Tightly Shut

In the second half of 1864, both the federal Congress and military tried to reduce illicit trade with the Confederacy. However, even as they were making progress toward curtailment, President Lincoln implemented policies to open interbelligerent trade wider than ever.

The Purchasing Act of July 2, 1864, which prohibited naval prize law on inland waters, also required that the initial buyers of items originating behind Confederate lines be employees (agents) of the US Treasury, as opposed to private citizens. (Previously the Treasury exclusively granted a limited number of private citizens authority to go beyond enemy lines, where they could buy cotton and other produce, transport it back to the Union side, and sell it on the open market.) As explained in chapter 2, Lincoln circumvented the intent of the Purchasing Act by specifying the manner in which Treasury Department regulations were to be applied. As implemented, Treasury rules applicable to the act permitted anyone delivering cotton to Treasury agents to be paid a greenback currency price equal to three-fourths of the market quote in New York.

Since greenbacks were not backed by gold, they traded at a significant markdown to specie. The discount was 60 percent in summer 1864.[1] Nonetheless, they were generally more valuable than

Confederate money. Lincoln reasoned that a proliferation of greenbacks within the rebellious regions would promote loyalty to his government.

Thus, any Northerner could become a "cotton trader" by infiltrating into the Confederacy, purchasing cotton at whatever price might be arranged, and delivering it to Treasury buyers at depots such as Memphis and New Orleans, where the sales price was 75 percent of the New York market quote. Finally, after the transaction, sellers were authorized to return to the Confederacy with noncontraband supplies equal to one-third of the value the cotton sold to the Treasury agent. The ultimate consumers of cotton, such as the New England mills, were provided opportunities to buy the inventories thus accumulated in the depot cities at periodic auctions.

Lincoln's provision enabling traders to return to the Confederacy with supplies equal to one-third of the value of the sold cotton enabled traders to pyramid profits for two reasons. First, a great many noncontraband supplies, including food and clothing, were desperately needed by Confederate armies. At the time there was no clear definition of "contraband." Second, the prices of the supplies traders were allowed to return beyond enemy lines were much higher in the Confederacy than in occupied depot cities. For example, bacon was only 22 cents a pound in Memphis but could bring six dollars a pound behind Rebel lines. Thus, traders returning with valued merchandise could use the supplies to purchase more cotton than they could afford on the previous trip. Therefore, accumulated profits would grow in a compounding manner following each round-trip.[2]

Lincoln found a second loophole to the restrictions of the Purchasing Act. Article 55 of the July 29, 1864, Treasury regulations stipulated that cotton previously bought and paid for could be brought within Union lines. The president and authorized Treasury officials could issue permits for such transport. Lincoln signed about forty. Those with his signature were more valued than ordinary Treasury Department permits and were sometimes sold, or even sublet. Such permits also enabled holders to sell their cotton at the full market price as opposed to the 25 percent discount otherwise required by the Purchasing Act.[3]

One permit issued by Treasury Secretary Fessenden was for thirty-five hundred bales in Mississippi for the seemingly ubiquitous William Butler. Another permit held by the Belgian consul in New Orleans authorized the diplomat to remove about twenty-three thousand bales. But in many instances the military blocked such movements. Evidently, several commanders were emboldened by the stance of Ulysses Grant, whose antitrade viewpoint became more influential after his appointment earlier in the year as the first US lieutenant general since George Washington, when Grant was simultaneously made general in chief. On September 13, Grant telegraphed Stanton, "[T]he amount of support received by our enemies through either the corruption of Treasury agents and post commanders is fearful, and should be stopped in some way."[4] Whether they knew of the wire to Stanton or not, most army generals were aware of Grant's hostility to trading with the enemy.

In any event, General Stephen Hurlbut told the Belgian consul that the military situation simply did not allow him to comply with Fessenden's permit. In New Orleans, General Canby seized all cotton entering his lines for later adjudication. Hurlbut, Canby, and other commanders effectively ignored Lincoln's directive strictly forbidding army or navy interference with cotton transactions applicable to Article 55.[5]

Consequently, on September 24, when Lincoln and Fessenden drew up Treasury procedures applicable to the Purchasing Act, they included a provision that any army or navy personnel interfering with the transportation of goods in either direction would be guilty of a military offense and punished accordingly. Treasury agents were instructed to accept applications from anyone saying they owned "or controlled" products beyond the lines. Such persons were to be granted a certificate identifying the goods to be conveyed, and agents were to request safe conduct for certificate holders. Finally, the procedures were to become effective when promulgated by the secretaries of war and the navy. War Secretary Stanton complied by October 6, but Navy Secretary Welles delayed until December 1.[6]

The delayed dissemination and other military steps used to restrict interbelligerent trade in the second half of 1864 frustrated Lincoln. He was particularly sensitive to the fact that, as in the Confederacy, cotton was an indispensible prop to the Union government's currency. In a letter to General Canby, Lincoln explained, "The way cotton goes now carries as much gold out of the country as to leave us [only] paper currency . . . [which] is so far depreciated as that for every hard dollar's worth of supplies we obtain, we contract to pay two-and-a-half dollars hereafter."[7]

The president was arguing that Fessenden's Treasury requirement that cotton be purchased with greenbacks instead of specie would reduce the outflow of the nation's gold reserves that were so vital to its international financial status. Senator Wilson of Massachusetts commented in support of Lincoln's point by noting that US gold reserves declined about $5 million to $6 million to pay for overseas imports during autumn 1864, when generals like Canby and Hurlbut had curtailed between-the-lines trading.[8]

The floodgates opened after the military rules were promulgated. During the first two weeks of operation at Memphis alone, certificates were issued for nearly forty thousand bales. General Washburn, who was the brother of Illinois congressman Elihu Washburne, complained that the system was widely abused. (The brothers spelled their surnames differently.) He did not believe that one man in a hundred who claimed to own (or control) cotton behind the lines actually did own (or control) a single bale. He estimated that Memphis Treasury purchasing agent George Ellery had issued hundreds of fraudulent permits. In New Orleans, General Canby wrote sarcastically that the local Treasury agent had been so busy issuing permits that "every bale of cotton in the Rebel lines is covered by permits."[9]

Ellery used other methods of leveraging his authority for personal gain. One was an illegal technique of enabling cotton sellers to avoid the mandatory 25 percent price discount to the New York cotton quote required by the Purchasing Act. For a fee, he would simply buy the cotton at 75 percent of the New York quote for a government account as required, but immediately resell it to those he bought it from for the same price. They could then sell it on the open market at the full New York quoted price. Evidently, Ellery felt that he should get his share of the largesse after discovering that others of higher rank were doing the same. For example, one merchant told Ellery that getting cotton out of the parts of Mississippi under the command of General Dana was accomplished by paying a fee to an attorney recommended by Dana's headquarters staff. The pertinent incident involved a fee of $25,000, but it was apparently a routine practice within Dana's domain.[10]

Leonard Swett, who helped engineer Lincoln's 1860 presidential nomination in Chicago, received three permits in December 1864 for one hundred fifty thousand bales. Swett's permits unrealistically covered cotton in every Confederate state except North Carolina and Virginia. Georgia planter Samuel Noble received a permit for two hundred fifty thousand bales. New Yorker Hanson Risley, who supervised all depot city Treasury agents, approved Noble's application. When questioned by a congressional investigating committee, Risley explained that Lincoln's bodyguard, Ward Hill Lamon, accompanied Noble and that the president also recommended the Southerner. In the three months from November 1864 through January 1865, Risley issued permits totaling nine hundred thirty thousand bales.[11] Most of the recipients were men recommended by Lincoln or New York political boss Thurlow Weed, who was also a thirty-year political ally of Secretary of State Seward.[12]

Risley's acquaintance with Seward also predated the war. After the war, Seward became infatuated with Risley's daughter Olive, who was in her mid-twenties when the secretary was in his late sixties. In an effort to stop tongues wagging, Seward adopted Olive when he was seventy years old.

Ward Hill Lamon recommended his own brother, Robert, for three permits totaling fifty thousand bales. One of Robert's Chicago business partners, James Patterson, wrote Ward Lamon that a permit holder told him "such permits are obtained by proper influences" and asked that Ward provide Patterson a permit in Robert's name. Patterson concluded, "I can make more money than a jackass can carry, but it must be through your instrumentality." Ward

Lamon became a part of the scheme and soon sought permits of his own. In his request, he reminded the president of the administration's "unceasing . . . [determination] to deprive the Confederacy of its greatest element of material strength and . . . to make . . . cotton the basis of this government's currency: for cotton is gold."[13]

Even Vice President Hannibal Hamlin (replaced by Andrew Johnson on the 1864 ticket) sought to profit from intersectional trade. Expecting to share in the proceeds, Hamlin asked Lincoln to provide a 23,640-bale permit to Fergus Penniston authorizing him to transport the cargo through enemy lines into Union-controlled territory. Lincoln obliged with a note advising all army, navy, and civil officers to provide Penniston "all the facilities that may be required to carry out the design of this permit."[14]

Few Northerners were better able to gain cotton-trading favors than Thurlow Weed. He had a well-earned reputation for influence peddling and profiteering. Lincoln was anxious to win New York in the 1864 presidential election because his margin in the state four years earlier was only seven thousand votes. In September 1864, one of Lincoln's private secretaries, John Nicolay, reported learning that Weed intended to raise money for the president's campaign by dealing in cotton.[15]

That same month, a Weed associate named Draper was appointed customs collector for the port of New York. In December, when General William T. Sherman occupied Savannah, where nearly forty thousand cotton bales were warehoused,[16] Draper was sent to the city to take charge of the supply. Navy Secretary Welles was "sickened." He complained, "The mission of Draper will be a swindle. A [preferential] ring will be formed for the purchase of the cotton, regardless of public or private rights." Presumably, Welles believed that the ring would be permitted to buy the cotton on bargain terms. Weed had a long association with fellow New Yorker Risley, who had wide powers to negotiate cotton-purchasing contracts. Some of the contracts were arranged at Weed's headquarters in room 11 of the Astor House in New York.[17] The New York Chamber of Commerce "reminded" the federal government that Southerners owed the businessmen of New York City unsettled accounts from the early days of secession amounting to $150 million.[18]

After occupying Savannah, General Sherman could attest to the veracity of a Mark Twain aphorism: "None but an ass pays a compliment and asks a favor at the same time. There are many asses."[19] The general was almost immediately swamped with compliments for his "march to the sea" and flooded with gifts from the North, including cases of fine bourbon, and Humboldt cigars along with invitations to visit elegant New York homes. Some favor seekers were more subtle, and perhaps more successful. Among them might have been those approaching the general through his brother John, who was a senator from Ohio. For example, the senator provided a written introduction for one Daniel Rees, explaining that Rees had "been a fast friend & contributed to my election as Senator." Given that cotton was trading at about a dollar per pound in December 1864, Savannah's forty thousand bales were worth about $20 million, which is equivalent to almost $300 million in 2013 dollars.[20]

The temptation among Northern politicians to use influence for profit in cotton trading during the last year of the war proved irresistible to a number of people with otherwise constructive reputations. Among them were some who are highly regarded by modern historians. One example is Thomas Corwin, who had been a governor of Ohio and one of its US senators. He had also served for a time as Treasury secretary under Millard Fillmore.

As minister to Mexico, Corwin significantly aided the Union war effort by keeping the ultimately ascendant Liberal Party under Benito Juarez mostly allied with Lincoln's government. Although he persistently dangled unfulfilled proposals of monetary aid to Juarez, Corwin was decidedly more effective than his Confederate counterpart, John Pickett, who was recalled by Richmond after compiling an embarrassing record. But Corwin's tendency for influence peddling also surfaced as he was serving in Mexico. One of his first acts was to negotiate a monopolistic pact for regular steamship service between New York and Veracruz through a line in which he was a part owner.[21]

In September 1864, Lincoln's friend William Butler commented, "old Tom Corwin has squat at the door of the Treasury & through [Assistant Treasury Secretary George] Harrington is levying blackmail at a fearful rate." Harrington was a long-time Treasury Department employee and worked for Corwin when the latter was secretary of the Treasury. When Corwin and Harrington tried to make Butler pay $10,000 for a cotton-trading permit, Lincoln's friend declined and warned he would complain to the president if the two refused to execute the papers without a bribe. Butler claimed that Harrington was a partner in the Memphis cotton brokerage of E. Parkman, Brooks, & Company, which was given a permit for fifteen thousand bales exempted from the restrictions of the Purchasing Act. Within less than two months, Confederate General Kirby Smith reported the same firm offered to buy fifteen thousand cotton bales directly from him at the bargain price of thirty cents per pound in specie when the market price was over one dollar per pound. Kirby Smith said Parkman "brings the authority of the President and Secretary of the Treasury of the United States for the transaction."[22]

Later, Corwin admitted he obtained a fifteen-thousand-bale permit for Parkman. He also acknowledged that he secured a permit for Texas military governor Andrew J. Hamilton, who was previously involved in questionable between-the-lines trading. Finally, Corwin was the attorney for notorious contraband trader George Lane, who patronized General Butler, a virtuoso of interbelligerent trade. Characteristic of patterns established earlier in the war at New Orleans, the general's own brother-in-law was a business partner to Lane.[23]

Another politician-turned-lobbyist who attempted to profit late in the war was former Illinois senator Orville Browning. He was an old Lincoln friend who had been appointed to fill the seat of Stephen Douglas, who died of illness in summer 1861. Browning failed to keep his seat in the November 1862 general election when a wave of antiwar sentiment swept the states north of the Ohio River. In the last months of the war, Browning schemed to buy sizable quantities of tobacco and cotton in Richmond and Wilmington in partnership with another Illinois politician, James Singleton. Since they proposed to use greenbacks, Lincoln did not object. Unfortunately for Browning and Singleton, the Confederacy collapsed before they could complete their transaction. The Rebel produce that had been inventoried for them behind enemy lines went up in smoke as the Confederate armies evacuated.[24]

Singleton represented himself as a private peace emissary. He claimed to have met with "Rebel Commissioners" in Canada in November 1864. Singleton told Browning they informed him that Lincoln might be able to negotiate surrender terms that would include extinction of the Confederacy by reunification. Given Browning's introduction, Singleton asked Lincoln for permission to travel to Richmond to learn if such terms were realistically attainable. Singleton claimed to have reached Richmond, where he said that there was a large sentiment for liberal surrender terms but that Davis and other leaders would not agree. He so informed the president on returning, but added that he also contracted to buy large amounts of tobacco with greenbacks.

Singleton claimed Lincoln replied that he "wanted to get out all [the tobacco and cotton] he could, and send in all the greenbacks he could in exchange." According to Singleton, Lincoln further explained that such trade would benefit impoverished Southerners and encourage them to seek peace with reunion. The president instructed Risley to give Singleton a pass and informed General Grant that he approved of Singleton's enterprise. Upon hearing rumors that Singleton was actually going to supply Lee's army with bacon, Grant seized a tobacco shipment erroneously thought to be Singleton's and asked that the permit be revoked. Bowing to a rising volume of complaints from Grant and others, Lincoln gave Grant authority to unilaterally prohibit between-the-lines trading anywhere east of the Appalachians. Consequently, Singleton was blocked and soon sank into obscurity.[25]

By January 1865, the US Congress became sufficiently frustrated to launch a joint Senate-House investigation of trade with the Confederacy. The results were reported on March 1, 1865, by Illinois congressman Washburne, who was one of Grant's political proponents from the earliest days of the war. The conclusions of the

House report, *Trade With the Rebellious States,* were condemning. Intersectional trade was described as a "disgraceful scramble for wealth" that prolonged the war and "cost thousands of lives." Although apparently sanctioned under the letter of the law, much of the trade was "for the use of Rebel armies." The report recommended more restrictive legislation, which was adopted two days later with only three dissenting votes in the Senate and none in the House. The bill was intended to shut down trade until the end of the war. Given the one-sided favorable votes in the Senate and House, nearly everyone was surprised when Lincoln rejected it by pocket veto.[26]

Secretary of the Treasury Hugh McCulloch, who was appointed by Abraham Lincoln five weeks before his assassination. (*Library of Congress*)

As the war approached an end, America's cotton market became a shameful feeding frenzy of greed dominated by abuse of power concentrated in the hands of a comparative few who in the full judgment of history are nearly indistinguishable from thieves. A month before Lee's surrender at Appomattox, Hugh McCulloch was appointed Lincoln's third Treasury secretary. He soon despairingly observed, "I am sure that I sent some honest cotton agents South, but it sometimes seems very doubtful that any of them remained honest very long."[27] The restraints were too weak compared to the rewards, while the temptations were overpowering.

Upon securing an appointment, a dishonest Treasury purchasing agent was practically granted a license to steal. As historian Robert Selph Henry discovered, "an alert, hard-working and reasonably ingenious cotton agent could earn for himself as much as $80,000 a month—[making] the $25,000 which one deputy agent admitting paying for his commission seem like a pretty good speculation."[28]

At the end of the war, an estimated five million bales lay inventoried in the South. US Treasury agents sent throughout the South to take possession of "abandoned" property and items owned by the Confederate government seized about three million bales. Although the prime aim was to collect cotton, the agents would grab whatever could be sold. Historian Merton Coulter summed up a number of swindles:

> The brazen dishonesties practiced by these agents almost surpass belief. . . . In Savannah alone, out of $21 million worth of cotton sold, they handed over to the U. S. Treasury only $8 million. . . . An agent in Texas forced a woman to sell for $75 a bale her 400 bales worth $200 each. . . . Another agent who had an interest in a steamboat refused to let a planter move his cotton unless he shipped it on the agent's craft.
>
> . . . [T]wo of the greatest cotton thieves were Simon Draper, general cotton agent for the Atlantic and Gulf states, with headquarters in New York City, and William P. Mellen, agent for the interior with offices in Cincinnati. They seized cotton indiscriminately and then allowed the owner to recover part for a quitclaim on the remainder... Draper, who had been bankrupt when he received his appointment, became a millionaire after a few years. . . . William Chandler, Assistant Secretary of the Treasury, in charge of cotton seizures, entered upon his work poor, but emerged worth hundreds of thousands of dollars. Many got rich, few were punished.[29]

During the final months of the war, desperate conditions in the South also led humanitarian instincts to authorize trade that might otherwise have been denied. In one instance, Lincoln was approached directly by a Baptist minister, Rev. Thomas Teasdale, who was a representative of the Mississippi State Orphans Home. Before the war, Teasdale had served temporarily at a church in Lincoln's hometown and was warmly recognized by the president.

Teasdale asked permission to ship cotton purchased with Confederate money through the lines to New York, where it could be sold to purchase supplies for the orphanage. The pastor formalized his request by presenting a petition by the orphanage board describing the impoverished conditions and endorsed on the back by

President Jefferson Davis. Evidently offended by the Davis endorsement, Lincoln responded by explaining that economic shortages were intentionally employed to motivate Southerners "to give up this wicked rebellion." Teasdale replied that "the hapless little ones" were not perpetrators of the war but merely victims of it. Lincoln softened, replying, "That is true and I must do something for you."[30]

Lincoln wrote a note to General Canby in New Orleans, authorizing—but not ordering—the general to accommodate Teasdale. The president then endorsed the back of the orphanage petition, encouraging the secretaries of war and the Treasury to meet with Teasdale regarding his "praiseworthy effort." Lincoln wrote his endorsement below that of Davis, thereby transforming the document into perhaps the only one to have the signatures of both Davis and Lincoln in their capacities as presidents.[31]

On May 22, 1865, thirty-seven days after taking office following Lincoln's assassination, President Andrew Johnson announced that all Southern ports, except a few in Texas, would no longer be blockaded and instead be freely open to commerce on July 1. Europe was eager to buy cotton, and Southerners badly needed the potential revenues from their once-mighty cash crop. But it was not to be. Instead of a flow of money in and cotton out, the hopeful scenario vanished owing to ravenously greedy politicians, corrupted Treasury employees, and dishonorable military commanders.

Under an act of May 9, 1865, lawful sales of cotton were burdened with extra fees. For example, there was a 25 percent fee for cotton that had been raised by slaves, in addition to a revenue and transportation tax. Even if the cotton were raised by free labor, there was still a revenue tax of 2.5 cents per pound and a transportation fee of 4 cents per pound. The tax and fee were paid by the producer merely for the privilege of moving his cotton to market. Cotton inventories owned by the Confederate government, or due to the Rebel government under taxes-in-kind or tithes previously applicable in the Confederacy, were forfeited to the US Treasury.

Identification of bales into the proper categories was subject to various frauds. For example, whether the cotton was "Confederate" or "private" was often questionable. "Debates" were often decided against private owners unless they paid a bribe to a Treasury agent. But the method could be expensive because a number of agents and military commanders took such bribes sequentially in the same regions. A second abuser may choose to deny the validity of the certificate issued by the first, thereby leaving the owner with little choice but to pay a second bribe with no ability to obtain a refund for the first one. Sometimes legitimate owners had to find a local rogue who had been recognized as loyal to the Union during the war to officially swear that he was the true owner of the cotton while secretly demanding a split in the proceeds when the cotton was sold.[32]

Another deceitful method was to "pluck" cotton under shipment. A toll was taken on bales sent to market by removing cotton from each bale while misleadingly delivering the specified number of bales. For example, a five-hundred-pound bale leaving the gin might only weigh three hundred pounds at its destination, but would still be falsely represented as a full bale upon delivery. Under this scenario, the loser was the Treasury, which received undersized cotton bales. A variation of the technique was to assign only bales of the poorest quality cotton to the federal government while reserving the best quality bales for buyers willing to pay a bribe or make some similar arrangement to share profits with a Treasury agent.[33]

A culture of abuse became acceptable for those with power and influence. Tennessee journalist Harvey Watterson wrote to President Johnson, "So many parties, official and unofficial, were engaged in stealing cotton" that it was impossible to know how much was stolen. The more famous Whitelaw Reid of the *New York Tribune,* who toured the South at the close of the war wrote "the practice [is to regard] everything left in the [defeated South] as the legitimate prize of the first officer who discovers it. . . . In general, our people seem to go upon the theory that, having conquered the country, they are entitled to the best it has, and [are] duty bound to use as much of it as possible."[34]

Cotton previously owned by the Confederate government was supposed to be sent only to designated agents in New York and

Cincinnati, where it was to be sold and the proceeds deposited in the Treasury. It is estimated that as many as three million bales were seized from the South up to the middle of 1866. Given prices prevailing at the time, the value of such a quantity should have been about $400 million to $500 million. Instead, the Treasury realized only about $30 million from the fraction of about one hundred fifteen thousand bales that survived the twisted ordeal of bribery, corruption, fraud, and theft.[35]

“Picking cotton near Montgomery, Alabama,” a photograph from the Civil War era. (*Library of Congress*)

# CONCLUSION

THE LENGTH AND SCALE OF THE CIVIL WAR RADICALLY TRANSformed the American economy. As Table 3 indicates (overleaf), total federal government spending in the last year of the war was over sixteen times as great as in the first year. From 1860 to 1865, the gross national product increased from $4.3 billion to $9.9 billion, which translates to an 18 percent compounded annual growth rate. Furthermore, since the economy in the South was shrinking, the growth rate applicable to the Northern states was probably well above 20 percent annually. Despite the abundance of death and sacrifice among the soldiers, it was a time of unprecedented prosperity in the North. As a result, after the war, the North was far less economically reliant on the South than previously. Of course, nobody knew that would be the result when the war started.

In antebellum America, the economies of the North and South were much more interdependent. Lincoln correctly observed in his first inaugural address that commerce between the two sections could not abruptly end.

Since its economy depended primarily on cash crops such as cotton and tobacco, the South relied on the states northwest of the Ohio River for provender and customarily purchased much of its manufactured goods from states in the Northeast. Similarly, the economy in the North depended on the South for cotton and its massive exports that supported important Northern commercial sectors such as shipping, finance, insurance, warehousing, and other services connected with cotton finance and maritime trade. Centered in New England, cotton textiles was the country's biggest manufacturing industry and obtained almost all its raw materials from the South. About 80 percent of the nation's exports originated in the South, and cotton alone accounted for two-thirds of it. Without Southern exports, America would have been required to reduce imports in order to avoid an unfavorable trade balance. Such a reduction would have cut customs duties, which were the chief source of federal tax revenue. In 1860, total federal taxes were $65 million, of which $53 million (82 percent) were from tariffs.[1]

TABLE 3

United States Government Revenues and Spending, 1860–1865
(In Millions of Dollars)

| | 1860 | 1861 | 1862 | 1863 | 1864 | 1865 |
|---|---|---|---|---|---|---|
| Tax Revenue | 65 | 50 | 60 | 124 | 277 | 348 |
| Deficit Spending | 13 | 30 | 425 | 602 | 601 | 963 |
| Total Spending | 78 | 80 | 485 | 726 | 878 | 1,311 |

Source: http://www.usgovernmentspending.com

Consequently, the monetary volume of intersectional trade that continued while the two sides were fighting the four-year Civil War remained important. Owing to the widespread bribery, fraud, smuggling, and theft characteristic of the shadowy commerce, it is difficult to know how much cotton the North obtained from the South during the war. However, despite the higher profile in our public memory for blockade-runners like the fictional Rhett Butler, economist Stanley Lebergott concluded the amount of cotton exported to Europe through the blockade was only about half as much as what was traded through enemy lines to the Northern states, which he estimated at nine hundred thousand bales.[2]

Lebergott's estimate is probably low, however. The ports of Boston and New York alone imported nine hundred thousand bales during the war. Of that amount, only one hundred sixty thousand came from Great Britain and little arrived from Brazil and the West Indies.[3] Thus, about seven hundred forty thousand bales must have come from occupied Southern ports such as New Orleans, or blockade-running centers like Nassau and Bermuda. At a minimum, it is necessary to increase the seven hundred forty thousand by adding the number of bales shipped north from the hinterlands from depots such as Memphis. Lebergott estimated hinterland trade at over six hundred thousand bales. So the two components (600,000 + 740,000) total more than 1.3 million bales.[4]

Other sources point to similar estimates. For example, in *Federal Trade with the Confederate States,* Robert Futrell estimated that almost nine hundred thousand bales went North during the three years from 1862 to 1864. On March 1, 1865, a House Committee investigation concluded that "not less" than two million bales had been contracted for, although not necessarily yet delivered, under Treasury regulations adopted less than a year earlier, in July 1864.[5] Finally, cotton smuggled into the North without permits was unreported, thereby implying that reported statistics necessarily understate the total volume.

Considering all factors, it seems likely that at least 1.25 million bales of cotton were shipped from the South to the North during the war. Assuming the ultimate buyer paid seventy-five cents per pound, the total value was over $465 million, which equates to about $7.1 billion in 2013 dollars.[6] Based on the 1860 US population of 31.4 million, the $7.1 billion is equivalent to about $225 per person. By comparison, an economic sector averaging $225 per capita for the 2010 census population of 309 million would total $69 billion, which is nearly twice the size of the $38 billion in auto sales by all US dealers in 2012.[7]

Most of the value for the wartime intersectional trade was due to inflated cotton prices resulting from shortages. For example, the seventy-five cents-per-pound price assumed in the $465 million figure noted above compares to a prewar price of thirteen cents, as indicated in Table 2 in chapter 1. Similarly, only about two million bales departed the Confederacy through a combination of exports and interbelligerent trade during the war, whereas antebellum peacetime production implies that a normal four-year period would have totaled about 18 million bales. Thus, the drop in physical volume during the war was probably over 85 percent.

There can be little doubt that interbelligerent trade was of greater benefit to the South than to the North and that it prolonged the war. In 1864, Senator John Ten Eyck of New Jersey stated, "Under the permission to trade, supplies have not only gone in, but bullets and powder, instruments of death, which our heroic soldiers have been compelled to face . . . upon almost every field . . . in which they have been engaged in the South."[8] As noted, the 1865 congressional investigating committee determined that trade with the Confederacy "is believed to have led to the prolongation of the War and cost the country thousands of lives and millions upon millions of treasure."[9] Historian Sellew Roberts estimated it lengthened the war by a year.[10] Historian James Ford Rhodes concluded:

> If accurate statistics could be obtained it would surprise [no one] that the North received more cotton from the internal commerce than did Great Britain from the blockade-runners; the greater portion of this staple came from a region under control of the . . . Confederacy. . . . This trade was a greater advantage to the South than to the North. . . . [T]he South obtained salt, quinine, powder, and arms, absolute necessaries for carrying on the War.[11]

Despite numerous complaints from military officers, Lincoln allowed the trade to continue until the end of the war. In response to objections from General Edward Canby, the president answered that higher cotton prices caused by scarcity enabled the Confederacy to acquire as much specie as prior to the war by exporting only a small fraction of the antebellum tonnage. He reasoned it was better to let Northern commercial interests buy and transship the cotton to Europe than to permit the Rebels to do it directly. He closed his letter to Canby with a specious argument borrowed from New England textile baron Edward Atkinson: "[It is] better to give [the enemy] guns for [cotton], than to let him, as now, get both guns and ammunition, for it." In assessing the president's explanation, historian James McPherson wrote, "Lincoln's rationalization did not satisfy [Canby], nor does it fully satisfy the historian."[12]

Yet owing to his roots as a Whig capitalist, Lincoln had faith that the profit motive could work to the advantage of reunion. He believed that commerce was the glue that held the Union together. The more intersectional trade, the stronger the binding ties. "If pecuniary greed can be made to aid us in such effort," he said, "let us be thankful that so much good can be got out of pecuniary greed."[13]

He was consistently more lenient toward trade with the enemy than was either Congress or the military. When in the first year Congress gave him an act to restrict trade, he waited five weeks before implementing it because he wanted to craft procedures that would enable intersectional commerce to continue. When New York industrialist August Belmont opined in 1862 that cotton trade could weaken the Confederacy, Lincoln replied that he had been in agreement for some time. Even near the end of the war, he pocket vetoed a nearly unanimously passed bill intended to block nearly all trade. The president most frequently defended his permissive interbelligerent trade policy "for its bearing on our finances," by which he meant the conservation of Treasury gold reserves.[14]

Although the profit motive might serve as a glue to hold the country together, the privileged access required to exercise it in the cotton market was a tar baby to which each corrupting incident adhered. Historian William C. Harris concluded:

> Lincoln's trade policy may have contributed to Northern financial stability . . . but the abuses and corruption . . . including his granting of permits to Illinois associates, contributed to the decline of values that he held dear. . . . When it became clear in 1864 that the commerce had become a lucrative operation for dishonest and unpatriotic entrepreneurs and was helping to keep the rebellion alive, Lincoln . . . should have acted vigorously to

> end the trade. He did not. The erosion of moral standards . . . would become increasingly apparent during the postwar period. Some blame for this condition . . . should attach to Lincoln.[15]

The corruption that accompanied interbelligerent trade was scandalous. Government officials and even military officers were bribed to shut their eyes. In January 1863, Charles Dana, who was a special investigating agent for War Secretary Stanton, wrote from Memphis "the mania for . . . cotton has . . . corrupted and demoralized the army."[16] Five months later, Lincoln himself admitted to Illinois friend William Kellogg, "The officers of the army in numerous instances are believed to connive and share in the profits."[17] Historian Ludwell Johnson wrote that "cotton permits were sold on the streets of New York; soldiers were bribed; traders were blackmailed; Treasury agents were disgraced."[18]

Secretary Chase's agent in New Orleans repeatedly wrote he could not check "unwarranted" trade because it profited General Butler's elder brother, Andrew.[19] Lincoln was besieged by many politicians and business leaders seeking privileges and promoting schemes for cotton buying, including Ohio governor William Dennison, Illinois senator Orville Browning, former Whig associate James Singleton, Illinois attorney William Weldon, and New York political boss Thurlow Weed, among others.[20]

General Ulysses Grant's brother-in-law, Samuel Casey, was given a special permit signed by Lincoln to travel multiple times behind enemy lines to buy cotton and transport it back to the Union side. The Confederate government owned the cotton Casey sought, and he contracted to pay for it with British pounds even though US Treasury regulations at the time prohibited the use of anything but greenbacks. Lincoln's friend William Butler was a member of the Casey partnership.[21]

Bribery and misconduct were also rife on the Confederate side of intersectional trade. For example, cavalry officers might be bribed to prevent them from burning cotton that planters wanted to sell to Northern traders. Similarly, pickets were sometimes bribed to allow cotton to be transported beyond Confederate military lines.

However, such actions were less detrimental to the Confederate cause than the reciprocal conduct on the Northern side was to the Union.[22] That is because Southerners principally exchanged non-contraband items such as cotton, tobacco, and turpentine, whereas the Northerners traded supplies that enabled the Rebel armies to remain in the field, including weapons, munitions, medicine, and salt, among many others. In contrast, cotton sold to Northerners was typically consumed by the New England textile mills, which, beyond providing some clothing (uniforms were made mostly of wool rather than cotton) and tents, did little to sustain the Union armies. Nonetheless, intersectional trade had a demoralizing effect among Confederate citizens because it made a few wealthy, while the war impoverished nearly all others. One Southerner enriched by such trade was Richard King, who founded the famous King Ranch in Texas. He made a fortune on wartime Rio Grande trade and was granted a pardon after the war, like most ordinary Southerners.

There are at least two reasons that knowledge of Civil War trading with the enemy should be more widely understood. First, it is a neglected part of the whole story. Second, it prompts inquiry into the rarely investigated reasons why the North fought, as opposed to inquiry into why the cotton states seceded.

Contemporary historians almost unanimously deny that the war resulted from a general disagreement over states' rights. They correctly note that the chief right the cotton states wanted to protect was the right to slavery. But most fail to appreciate that it was the widely anticipated economic consequences of disunion that motivated influential politicians and businessmen in the North to "save the Union." The willingness to trade gold, weapons, munitions, and other contraband to the South in order to avoid such consequences underscores the importance that Lincoln attached to the North's need for intersectional trade. Although not without a humanitarian benefit to destitute Southerners, the bilateral commerce was mostly a bogus "need" for Northerners that unnecessarily protracted the war and lengthened the casualty lists.

# NOTES

## Introduction

1. Robert A. Jones, *Confederate Corsair* (Mechanicsburg, PA: Stackpole, 2000), 110.
2. Robert W. Delaney, "Matamoras: Port for Texas during the Civil War," *Southwestern Historical Quarterly* 58 (July 1954–April 1955): 480.
3. James W. Daddysman, *The Matamoros Trade* (Newark: University of Delaware Press, 1984), 108–113, 143.
4. John Mason Hart, "Stillman, Charles," *Handbook of Texas Online*, Texas State Historical Association, accessed July 29, 2013, http://www.tshaonline.org/handbook/online/articles/fst57; John Mason Hart, "Stillman, James," *Handbook of Texas Online,* Texas State Historical Association, http://www.tshaonline.org/handbook/online/articles/fstbp; Daddysman, *Matamoros Trade,* 157–158.
5. Chester G. Hearn, *When the Devil Came Down to Dixie* (Baton Rouge: Louisiana State University Press, 1997), 196.
6. M. A. DeWolfe Howe, ed., *Home Letters of General Sherman* (New York: Charles Scribner's Sons, 1909), 232.
7. Robert F. Futrell, "Federal Trade with the Confederate States: 1861–1865" (PhD diss., Vanderbilt University, 1950), 83–102.
8. Gay Talese, *The Kingdom and the Power* (New York: Bantam, 1969), 191.
9. *Chicago Daily Times*, December 10, 1860, "The Editorials of Secession Project," American Historical Association, accessed July 29, 2013, http://historians.org/projects/secessioneditorials/Editorials/ChicagoTimes_12_10_60.htm.
10. Abraham Lincoln, presidential inaugural address, March 4, 1861, Joint Congressional Committee on Inaugural Ceremonies, accessed December 15, 2013, http://www.inaugural.senate.gov/swearing-in/address/address-by-abraham-lincoln-1865.

11. Gene Dattel, *Cotton and Race in the Making of America* (Lanham, MD: Ivan R. Dee, 2009), 82.
12. Charles Adams, *When in the Course of Human Events* (Lanham, MD: Rowman & Littlefield, 2000), 24–25.
13. Futrell, "Federal Trade," 24.
14. Ludwell Johnson, "Trading with the Union: The Evolution of Confederate Policy," *Virginia Magazine of History and Biography* 78, no. 3 (July 1970): 310–311.
15. Phil Leigh, "Trading with the Enemy," *New York Times* Opinionator, October 28, 2012, accessed July 29, 2013, http://opinionator.blogs.nytimes.com/2012/10/28/trading-with-the-enemy/.
16. Ludwell Johnson, *North against South: The American Iliad 1848–1877* (Columbia, SC: Foundation for American Education, 1995, orig. publ. as *Division and Reunion: 1848–1877*, New York: John Wiley and Sons, 1978), 117.
17. William Brooksher, *War along the Bayous* (Dulles, VA: Brassey's, 1998), 3; William H. Nulty, *Confederate Florida: The Road to Olustee* (Tuscaloosa: University of Alabama Press, 1990), 60.
18. Delaney, "Matamoros," 473–487.
19. Futrell, "Federal Trade," 78–84, 194–204.
20. Jones, *Confederate Corsair*, 110.
21. Stanley Lebergott, "Why the South Lost: Commercial Purpose in the Confederacy, 1861–1865," *Journal of American History* 70, no.1 (June 1983): 72–73.
22. Andrew J. Smith, *Starving the South* (New York: St. Martin's Press, 2011), 125–126.
23. Ludwell H. Johnson, "Contraband Trade during the Last Year of the Civil War," *Mississippi Valley Historical Review* 91, no. 4 (March 1963): 642.
24. Robert L. Kerby, *Kirby Smith's Confederacy* (Tuscaloosa: University of Alabama Press, 1972), 155–207.
25. Ludwell Johnson, "Northern Profit and Profiteers: The Cotton Rings of 1864–1865," *Civil War History* 12, no. 2 (June 1966): 103.
26. James Ford Rhodes, *The History of the Civil War, 1861–1865* (New York: Macmillan, 1917), 359.
27. Johnson, "Northern Profit," 101–115.
28. James McPherson, *Battle Cry of Freedom* (London: Oxford University Press, 1988), 622.
29. Merton E. Coulter, "Commercial Intercourse with the Confederacy in the Mississippi Valley, 1861–1865," *Mississippi Valley Historical Review* 5, no. 4 (March 1919): 388.

## Chapter One: The World Cotton Economy

1. Lauriston F. Bullard, "Lincoln's Conquest of New England," *Abraham Lincoln Quarterly* 2, no. 2 (June 1942): 53.
2. Charles Francis Adams Jr., *Richard Henry Dana* (Boston: Houghton, Mifflin, 1891), 127.
3. Ward Hill Lamon, *Recollections of Abraham Lincoln* (Cambridge, MA: University Press, 1911), 67.
4. Dattel, *Cotton and Race,* 36.
5. Ibid.
6. Frank Owsley, *King Cotton Diplomacy* (Chicago: University of Chicago Press, 1931), 8–9.
7. Dattel, *Cotton and Race,* 31–35.
8. Owsley, *King Cotton Diplomacy,* 2–4.
9. David Cohn, *The Life and Times of King Cotton* (New York: Oxford University Press, 1956), 17–18, 26; Dattel, *Cotton and Race,* 27–39.
10. Dattel, *Cotton and Race,* 82.
11. John Lockwood and Charles Lockwood, "First South Carolina. Then New York?," *New York Times* Opinionator, January 6, 2011, http://opinionator.blogs.nytimes.com/2011/01/06/first-south-carolina-then-new-york/?_r=0.
12. Dattel, *Cotton and Race,* 40–42.
13. Ibid., 39–50.
14. Ibid., 67.
15. Ibid., 61–85.
16. Orville Burton and Patricia Bonnin, "The Confederacy," *Macmillan Information Now Encyclopedia,* http://www.civilwarhome.com/kingcotton.htm.
17. Ronald Bailey, "Slavery Trade and the Development of Capitalism in the USA: The Textile Industry in New England," *Social Science History* 14, no. 3, 388–389.
18. Ibid., 389–390.
19. Thomas H. O'Connor, *Lords of the Loom* (New York: Charles Scribner's Sons, 1968), 9–18.
20. Stephen Yafa, *Cotton* (New York: Penguin, 2005), 105.
21. Bailey, "Slavery Trade," 395–396.
22. Ibid., 402–403.
23. O'Connor, *Lords of the Loom,* 50–55.
24. Anne Farrow, Joel Lang, and Jenifer Frank, *Complicity* (New York: Ballantine, 2005), 10–11.
25. Ibid.,12.

26. Ibid., 3.
27. Ibid.,15–23.
28. O'Connor, *Lords of the Loom,* 56–102.
29. Ibid., 104–141.
30. Cohn, *Life and Times,* 124.
31. Gary M. Walton and Hugh Rockoff, *History of the American Economy* (San Diego: Harcourt Brace Jovanovich, 1990), 346.
32. Cohn, *Life and Times,* 131.
33. Thomas H. O'Connor, "Lincoln and the Cotton Trade," *Civil War History* 7, no. 1 (March 1961): 32; David G. Surdam, *Northern Naval Superiority and the Economics of the American Civil War* (Columbia: University of South Carolina Press, 2001), 196.

## Chapter Two: Official Policy

1. Ludwell Johnson, "Trading with the Union: The Evolution of Confederate Policy," *Virginia Magazine of History and Biography* 78, no. 3 (July 1970): 310–311.
2. Stephen R. Wise, *Lifeline of the Confederacy* (Columbia: University of South Carolina Press, 1991), 12.
3. Futrell, "Federal Trade," 36.
4. Surdam, *Northern Naval Superiority,* 61–62.
5. Clement Eaton, *A History of the Southern Confederacy* (New York: Free Press, 1954), 139–141.
6. Johnson, "Trading with the Union," 308–325; Edward Pollard, *The Lost Cause* (Baltimore: E. B. Treat, 1883), 489.
7. Jerrold Northrop Moore, *Confederate Commissary General* (Shippensburg, PA: White Mane, 1996), 211.
8. Ibid., 187–189.
9. Ibid., 201–203.
10. Futrell, "Federal Trade," 88–90.
11. Dattel, *Cotton and Race,* 172.
12. Cohn, *Life and Times,* 125.
13. Richard Taylor, *Destruction and Reconstruction* (New York: De Capo, 1995), 235.
14. Congress of the Confederate States of America, *Statutes at Large,* ch. 25, An Act to Prohibit Dealing in the Paper Currency of the Enemy, February 6, 1864.
15. Gilder Lehrman Institute of American History, *Confederate Act to Authorize the Exportation of Produce and Merchandise,* accessed December 23, 2013, http://www.gilderlehrman.org/colletions/5905 34e9-fb05-44c7-a976- 099992402122?back=/mweb/search

%3Fpage%3D4%2526needle%3DTobacco%2520and%2520Smokin g%253B%2526fields%3D_t301001410.
16. Coulter, "Commercial Intercourse," 377–378.
17. O'Connor, "Lincoln and the Cotton Trade," 24.
18. Edward Bates, *Diary of Edward Bates* (Washington, DC: Government Printing Office, 1933), 265.
19. Orville Browning, *Diary of Orville Hickman Browning* (Springfield: Illinois State Historical Society, 1925), 563–564.
20. Thomas Boaz, *Guns for Cotton* (Shippensburg, PA: Burd Street Press, 1996), 2–3.
21. O'Connor, "Lincoln and the Cotton Trade," 20–21.
22. Dattel, *Cotton and Race,* 82.
23. William C. Harris, *Lincoln's Last Months* (Cambridge, MA: Harvard University Press, 2004), 177.
24. Futrell, "Federal Trade," 76.
25. Ibid., 128.
26. O'Connor, "Lincoln and the Cotton Trade," 26.
27. James Ford Rhodes, *The History of the United States from the Compromise of 1850 to the Restoration of Home Rule,* vol. 5 (New York: Harper & Brothers, 1899), 282.
28. John Niven, *Salmon P. Chase* (Oxford: Oxford University Press, 1995), 364–366, 374.
29. Futrell, "Federal Trade," 70.
30. Ludwell Johnson, *Red River Campaign* (Kent, OH: Kent State University Press, 1993), 53.
31. Rhodes, *History of the United States,* 5:301.
32. Albert Bushnell Hart, *Salmon Portland Chase* (Boston: Houghton, Mifflin, 1899), 228–229.
33. Coulter, "Commercial Intercourse," 385–388.
34. Ibid., 388–389.
35. McPherson, *Battle Cry,* 353, 356, 499, 500.
36. A. Sellew Roberts, "The Federal Government and Confederate Cotton," *American Historical Review* 32, no. 2 (January 1927): 267–268.
37. Willie Lee Rose, *Rehearsal for Reconstruction* (Athens: University of Georgia Press, 1999), 200–201.
38. Dean B. Mahin, *One War at a Time* (Washington, DC: Brassey's, 1999), 45–46.
39. Amanda Foreman, *A World on Fire: Britain's Crucial Role in the American Civil War* (New York: Random House, 2010), 821–822.
40. Mahin, *One War*, 45–46.

41. Ibid., 48.
42. Burton Hendrick, *Statesmen of the Lost Cause* (New York: Literary Guild, 1939), 274–275.

## Chapter Three: The Port Royal Experiment

1. Edward Atkinson, *Cheap Cotton by Free Labor* (Boston: H. W. Dutton, 1861), 1–5.
2. Ibid., 6.
3. Akiko Ochiai, *Harvesting Freedom* (Westport, CT: Praeger, 2004), 53.
4. Pollard, *Lost Cause,* 194.
5. Ochiai, *Harvesting Freedom,* 53–57, 60.
6. Rose, *Rehearsal,*105–108.
7. Akiko Ochiai, "The Port Royal Experiment Revisited," *New England Quarterly* 74, no. 1 (March 2001): 96.
8. Rose, *Rehearsal,* 205.
9. Ibid., 143.
10. Futrell, "Federal Trade," 155.
11. Ibid., 143–157.
12. Rose, *Rehearsal,* 204.
13. Ochiai, *Harvesting Freedom,* 87.
14. Ibid., 67–69.
15. Ibid., 69–70.
16. Ibid., 90, 97, 101.
17. Ibid., 95.
18. Ibid., 99.
19. Ochiai, "Port Royal Experiment," 97–99; Eric Foner, *Reconstruction* (New York: Harper & Row, 1988), 53.
20. Ochiai, "Port Royal Experiment," 106, 109.
21. Ibid., 114.
22. Michael Shapiro, "Rehearsal for Reconstruction," *New York Times* Opinionator, September 6, 2011, http://opinionator.blogs.nytimes.com/2011/11/06/rehearsal-for-reconstruction/.
23. Rose, *Rehearsal,* 269.
24. Ibid., 270.
25. Lawrence N. Powell, *New Masters* (New York: Fordham University Press, 1998), 34.
26. Foner, *Reconstruction,* 54; Rose, *Rehearsal,* 365; Powell, *New Masters*, 77, 147.

## Chapter Four: Matamoros

1. Delaney, "Matamoros," 474.
2. Wise, *Lifeline,* 86–89.
3. Marilyn Sibley, "Charles Stillman: A Case Study of Entrepreneurship on the Rio Grande, 1861–1865," *Southwestern Historical Quarterly* 77, no. 2 (October 1973): 232.
4. Ibid., 234.
5. Kerby, *Kirby Smith's Confederacy,* 178.
6. William Moss Wilson, "The Confederate of the Sierra Madre," *New York Times* Opinionator, September 1, 2011. http://opinionator.blogs. nytimes.com/2011/09/01/the-confederate-of-the-sierra-madre/.
7. James J. Horgan, "A Confederate Bull in a Mexican China Shop," in John M. Belohlavek and Lewis N. Wynne, eds., *Divided We Fall: Essays on Confederate Nation Building* (St. Leo, FL: St. Leo College Press, 1991), 74–75.
8. Henry Martyn Flint, *Mexico under Maximilian* (Philadelphia: National Publishing, 1867), 62–68.
9. Mahin, *One War,* 221–235.
10. Owsley, *King Cotton Diplomacy,* 109–119.
11. Ibid., 126.
12. Ronnie C. Tyler, "Cotton on the Border: 1861–1865," *Southwestern Historical Quarterly* 73, no. 4 (April 1970): 214.
13. Owsley, *King Cotton Diplomacy,* 140–145.
14. Daddysman, *Matamoros Trade,* 108–113, 143.
15. Delaney, "Matamoros," 473–487.
16. Ibid., 480, 473–487.
17. Alfred Hanna and Kathryn Hanna, *Napoleon III and Mexico* (Chapel Hill: University of North Carolina Press, 1971), 156–157.
18. Kerby, *Kirby Smith's Confederacy,* 182.
19. Daddysman, *Matamoros Trade,* 155–156, 158.
20. Ibid., 156–157.
21. Ibid., 157–158.
22. Sibley, "Charles Stillman," 228, 231.
23. Ibid., 239.
24. John Mason Hart, "Stillman, Charles," *Handbook of Texas Online*, Texas State Historical Association, www.tshaonline.org/handbook/online/articles/fst57; John Mason Hart, "Stillman, James." *Handbook of Texas Online*, Texas State Historical Association, www.tshaonline.org/handbook/online/articles/fstbp.

25. Peg Lamphier, *Kate Chase and William Sprague: Politics and Gender in a Civil War Marriage* (Lincoln: University of Nebraska Press, 2005), 46–47.
26. Ibid., 77–78.
27. Ibid., 95; Niven, *Chase,* 416.
28. Nathan Miller, *Theodore Roosevelt* (New York: William Morrow, 1992), 77.
29. Johnson, *Red River,* 19–21.
30. Ibid., 22–23.
31. Ibid., 49–78; Delaney, "Matamoros," 473–487; Hanna and Hanna, *Napoleon III,* 165–166.
32. Kerby, *Kirby Smith's Confederacy,* 377.
33. Mahin, *One War,* 185–187.
34. Wise, *Lifeline,* 184–186.

## Chapter Five: Mississippi Valley Trade

1. Futrell, "Federal Trade," 24.
2. Ibid., 67–70.
3. Surdam, *Northern Naval Superiority,* 184.
4. Futrell, "Federal Trade," 78.
5. Ibid., 74.
6. Ulysses Grant, *Personal Memoirs* (New York: De Capo, 1952), 207–208.
7. "Abraham Lincoln and Cotton," Lincoln Institute, accessed May 9, 2013, www.abrahamlincolnsclassroom.org/Library/newsletter.asp?ID=132&CRLI=180.
8. Futrell, "Federal Trade," 87–95.
9. O'Connor, "Lincoln and the Cotton Trade," 28.
10. Rhodes, *History of the United States,* 5:286.
11. Futrell, "Federal Trade," 108.
12. McPherson, *Battle Cry,* 622.
13. Futrell, "Federal Trade," 137.
14. Cohn, *Life and Times,* 129.
15. Brooks Simpson, *Ulysses S. Grant* (Boston: Houghton Mifflin, 2000), 164–166.
16. Charles Anderson Dana, *Recollections of the Civil War* (New York: D. Appleton, 1913), 18.
17. Johnson, "Northern Profit," 111–112.
18. Coulter, "Commercial Intercourse," 386.
19. *The War of the Rebellion: A Compilation of the Official Records of the Union and Confederate Armies* (Washington, DC: Government Printing Office, 1880), ser. 4, vol. 3, pt. 1, 282.

20. Futrell, "Federal Trade," 291–303; John B. Jones, *A Rebel War Clerk's Diary* (Philadelphia: J. B. Lippincott, 1866), 2:131.
21. Harris, *Lincoln's Last Months,* 177–179.
22. Bates, *Diary,* 276.
23. Browning, *Orville Hickman Browning,* 573, 578–579.
24. Futrell, "Federal Trade," 114–120.
25. Clement Eaton, *A History of the Southern Confederacy* (New York: Free Press, 1954), 241.
26. Carl H. Moneyhon, *The Impact of the Civil War and Reconstruction in Arkansas* (Baton Rouge: Louisiana State University Press, 1994), 130.
27. Thomas A. DeBlack, *With Fire and Sword* (Fayetteville: University of Arkansas Press, 2003), 86–87.
28. Ludwell Johnson, *North and South: The American Iliad, 1848–1877* (Columbia, SC: Foundation for American Education, 1993), 118.
29. Coulter, "Commercial Intercourse," 392.
30. Alan G. Bogue, *The Congressman's Civil War* (Cambridge: Cambridge University Press, 1988), 43.
31. Jones, *War Clerk's Diary,* 2:87.
32. Johnson, *Red River,* 10.
33. Ludwell H. Johnson, "The Butler Expedition of 1861–1862: The Profitable Side of War," *Civil War History* 11, no. 3 (September 1965): 230.
34. Ibid., 232–233.
35. Ibid., 234.
36. Ibid., 236.
37. Hearn, *Devil Came Down,* 196.
38. Ibid., 195.
39. Ibid.
40. Ibid., 107–134.
41. Ibid., 186.
42. O'Connor, "Lincoln and the Cotton Trade," 28.
43. Smith, *Starving the South,* 125, 119.
44. Futrell, "Federal Trade," 194–211.
45. Hearn, *Devil Came Down,* 187–189.
46. Johnson, *Red River,* 53.
47. Hearn, *Devil Came Down,* 184–185.
48. Roberts, "Federal Government," 267; Jones, *War Clerk's Diary,* 1:187.
49. Hearn, *Devil Came Down,* 192; Futrell, "Federal Trade," 211–213.

50. Coulter, "Commercial Intercourse," 387.
51. Roberts, "Federal Government," 272.
52. Johnson, *Red River,* 10–28.
53. Ibid., 52.
54. Ibid., 30.
55. Dattel, *Cotton and Race,* 212.
56. Ibid., 211.
57. Foner, *Reconstruction,* 54–56.
58. Carl H. Moneyhon, "From Slave to Free Labor: The Federal Plantation Experiment in Arkansas," in Anne J. Bailey and Daniel E. Sutherland, eds., *Civil War Arkansas* (Fayetteville: University of Arkansas Press, 2000), 178–179, 183; McPherson, *Battle Cry,* 711; Foner, *Reconstruction,* 54–56.
59. Dattel, *Cotton and Race,* 213–214.
60. Thomas W. Knox, *Campfire and Cotton Field* (New York: Bielock, 1865), 316; Bell Irvin Wiley, *Southern Negroes* (New York: Rinehart, 1938), 186.
61. Cohn, *Life and Times,* 128.
62. Powell, *New Masters,* 9, 11, 47.
63. Cohn, *Life and Times,* 126–127; Dattel, *Cotton and Race,* 216.
64. Powell, *New Masters,* 46.
65. Knox, *Campfire,* 320–321.
66. *Historical Statistics of the United States: Colonial Times to 1970,* pt. 1 Washington, DC, US Department of Commerce, Bureau of the Census), 518; Foner, *Reconstruction,* 58; Powell, *New Masters,* 7.
67. Powell, *New Masters,* 44, 146.

## Chapter Six: Abusing the Blockade

1. Boaz, *Guns for Cotton,* 7; Foreman, *World on Fire,* 80.
2. Mahin, *One War,* 164.
3. Clement Eaton, *A History of the Southern Confederacy* (New York: Free Press, 1954), 144; Thelma Peters, "Blockade-Running in the Bahamas during the Civil War," paper read May 5, 1943, before the Historical Association of Southern Florida, 20.
4. Peters, "Blockade-Running," 24–25.
5. Ibid., 19.
6. Boaz, *Guns for Cotton,* 61.
7. Smith, *Starving the South,* 127.
8. Ibid., 128; Greg Marquis, "The Ports of Halifax and St. Johns and the American Civil War," *(Canadian) Northern Mariner* 7, no. 1 (January 1998): 14.

9. Francis I. W. Jones, "This Fraudulent Trade" *(Canadian) Northern Mariner* 9, no. 4 (October 1999), 39.
10. Hamilton Cochran, *Blockade Runners* (Tuscaloosa: University of Alabama Press, 2005), 47.
11. Ibid., 63.
12. Ludwell H. Johnson, "Commerce between Northeastern Ports and the Confederacy: 1861–1865," *Journal of American History* 54, no. 1 (June 1967): 33.
13. Charles Cowley, *Leaves from a Lawyer's Life Afloat and Ashore* (Lowell, MA: Penhallow, 1879), 112–113.
14. Smith, *Starving the South,* 125–126.
15. Joseph T. Durkin, *Confederate Navy Chief* (Columbia: University of South Carolina Press, 1954), 170.
16. Glen N. Wiche, ed., *Dispatches from Bermuda: The Civil War Letters of Charles Maxwell Allen, US Consul to Bermuda, 1861–1888* (Kent, OH: Kent State University Press, 2009), 89.
17. Johnson, "Commerce between Northeastern Ports," 35.
18. Ibid., 30–33.
19. Ibid., 30–42; Niven, *Chase,* 351–352.
20. Robert Means Thompson and Richard Wainwright, *Confidential Correspondence of Gustavus Fox*, vol. 1 (New York: printed for the Naval History Society by De Vinne Press, 1918), 349; Merton E. Coulter. *The Confederate States of America: 1861–1865* (Baton Rouge: Louisiana State University Press, 1950), 289.
21. Jones, *War Clerk's Diary,* 1:310, 312, 358.
22. Ibid., 2:127, 179, 394.
23. Harris, *Lincoln's Last Months,* 182–183.
24. Kerby, *Kirby Smith's Confederacy,* 378.
25. Johnson, "Commerce between Northeastern Ports," 36–37.
26. Ibid., 35.
27. Johnson, "Contraband Trade," 640; Lamon, *Recollections of Abraham Lincoln,* 189.
28. Boaz, *Guns for Cotton,* 63; Owsley, *King Cotton Diplomacy,* 286; Cohn, *Life and Times,* 130.
29. Wise, *Lifeline,* 221.

## Chapter Seven: Norfolk

1. Ludwell Johnson, "Blockade or Trade Monopoly?," *Virginia Magazine of History and Biography* 93, no. 1 (January 1985): 54–56.
2. Kenneth Stampp, *And the War Came* (Baton Rouge: Louisiana State University Press, 1970), 81–82.

3. Peter Andreas, *Smuggler Nation* (Oxford: Oxford University Press, 2013), 173.
4. Johnson, "Blockade," 56–62.
5. Gideon Welles, *Diary*, vol. 1 (Boston: Houghton, Mifflin, 1911), 177.
6. Johnson, "Blockade," 62–69.
7. Ibid., 69–75.
8. Ibid., 75–76.
9. Welles, *Diary*, 165–167.
10. Johnson, "Blockade," 76–77.
11. Johnson, "Contraband Trade," 646.
12. Ibid., 643.
13. Ibid., 645.
14. Ibid., 642–643.
15. *The Record of Benjamin Butler from Original Sources* (Boston: pamphlet, 1883), 13.
16. Frederick A. Wallace, *Civil War Hero: George H. Gordon* (Charleston, SC: History Press, 2011), 98.
17. Ibid., 101; Futrell, "Federal Trade," 441.

## Chapter Eight: Kirby Smithdom

1. Surdam, *Northern Naval Superiority*, 177.
2. B. T. Johnson, "Memoir of the First Maryland Regiment," *Southern Historical Society Papers*, vol. 9, 482.
3. Simpson, *Grant*, 218.
4. Donald Miles, *Cinco de Mayo* (Lincoln, NE: iUniverse, 2006), 7–8.
5. Ibid., 132.
6. Gene Smith, *Maximilian and Carlota* (London: Harrap, 1973), 138.
7. Flint, Mexico under Maximilian, 67–68.
8. Smith, *Maximilian and Carlota*, 142.
9. Owsley, *King Cotton Diplomacy*, 539.
10. Ibid., 540.
11. Mahin, *One War*, 29–30.
12. Owsley, *King Cotton Diplomacy*, 546.
13. Mahin, *One War*, 223–224.
14. Ibid., 224–225.
15. Kerby, *Kirby Smith's Confederacy*, 187.
16. Johnson, *Red River*, 35.
17. Jones, *War Clerk's Diary*, 1:244.

18. Mahin, *One War,* 231–232.
19. Ibid., 233–234.
20. Owsley, *King Cotton Diplomacy,* 541–547.
21. Mahin, *One War,* 225.
22. Kerby, *Kirby Smith's Confederacy,* 189.
23. Fred Harrington, *Fighting Politician* (Westport, CT: Greenwood, 1948), 134–135.
24. Kerby, *Kirby Smith's Confederacy,* 191–198.
25. Alvin Josephy Jr., *The Civil War in the American West* (New York: Alfred A. Knopf, 1991), 223; Stephen Oates, "John S. 'Rip' Ford," *Southwestern Historical Quarterly* 64, no. 3 (January 1961): 308–309.
26. Johnson, *Red River,* 46, 49.
27. Johnson, "Northern Profit," 107; "Consumer Price Index (Estimate) 1800–," Federal Reserve Bank of Minneapolis, accessed August 5, 2013, www.minneapolisfed.org/community_education/teacher/calc/hist1800.cfm?.
28. Dattel, *Cotton and Race,* 203.
29. Johnson, *Red River,* 49, 64.
30. Kerby, *Kirby Smith's Confederacy,* 160.
31. Johnson, *Red River,* 7–8.
32. Ibid., 13–14.
33. Harris, *Lincoln's Last Months,* 182.
34. Johnson, *Red River,* 47–48.
35. Kerby, *Kirby Smith's Confederacy,* 160.
36. Ibid., 183.
37. Ibid., 173.
38. Daddysman, *Matamoros Trade,* 142–143.
39. Kerby, *Kirby Smith's Confederacy,* 173–207.
40. Michael B. Dougan, *Confederate Arkansas* (Tuscaloosa: University of Alabama Press, 1991), 120.
41. Johnson, *Red River,* 99–100, 171.
42. Curt Anders, *Disaster in Damp Sand* (Carmel, IN: Guild Press, 1997), 26.
43. Johnson, *Red River,* 65.
44. Judith Gentry, "John A. Stevenson: Confederate Adventurer," *Louisiana History* 35, no. 2 (1994): 155–159; Johnson, *Red River,* 64–65, 68–69.
45. Kerby, *Kirby Smith's Confederacy,* 274.
46. Johnson, "Northern Profit," 114.
47. Johnson, *Red River,* 72.

48. Ibid., 71–74.
49. Gary Dillard Joiner, *One Damn Blunder from Beginning to End* (Wilmington, DE: SR Books, 2003), 59.
50. Francis Lieber, *Lieber's Code and the Law of War* (Chicago: Precedent, 1983), 52.
51. Johnson, *Red River,* 76–78, 101–103.
52. Taylor, *Destruction*, 193.
53. Johnson, *Red River,* 253–254, 283; Michael Thomas Smith, *The Enemy Within* (Charlottesville: University Press of Virginia, 2011), 164.
54. Smith, *Enemy Within,* 164.
55. Coulter, "Commercial Intercourse," 392–393; Johnson, *Red River,* 285–287; *The Blockade Runners and Raiders* (Chicago: Time-Life Books, 1983), 91.
56. Smith, *Enemy Within,* 165.
57. Kerby, *Kirby Smith's Confederacy,* 389–390.
58. Ibid., 386–409.
59. Johnson, "Contraband Trade," 637–638.

## Chapter Nine: Eyes Tightly Shut

1. Futrell, "Federal Trade," 422.
2. David G. Surdam, "Traders or Traitors: Northern Cotton Trading During the Civil War," *Business and Economic History* 28, no. 2 (Winter 1999): 302.
3. Johnson, "Contraband Trade," 38–39.
4. Grant at City Point, Virginia, to Stanton, September 13, 1864, in Futrell, "Federal Trade," 437.
5. Futrell, 419–421.
6. Ibid., 423–424.
7. Lincoln to Canby, December 12, 1864, in Futrell, "Federal Trade," 431.
8. Futrell, "Federal Trade," 449.
9. Canby to Stanton, January 13, 1865, in Futrell, "Federal Trade," 434.
10. Johnson, "Northern Profits," 112.
11. Futrell, "Federal Trade," 445.
12. Surdam, "Traders or Traitors," 305.
13. Harris, *Lincoln's Last Months,* 181.
14. Ibid., 182.
15. Johnson, "Northern Profit," 103.
16. George Winston Smith, "Cotton from Savannah in 1865," *Journal of Southern History* 21, no. 4 (November 1955): 496.

17. Johnson, "Northern Profit," 103.
18. Smith, "Cotton from Savannah," 508.
19. Alex Ayers, *The Wit and Wisdom of Mark Twain* (New York: Meridian, 1989), 46.
20. Smith, "Cotton from Savannah," 497–498; "Consumer Price Index (Estimate) 1800–," Federal Reserve Bank of Minneapolis.
21. Miles, *Cinco de Mayo,* 6.
22. Johnson, "Northern Profits," 104.
23. Ibid., 105–106; Futrell, "Federal Trade," 439.
24. Browning, *Orville Hickman Browning,* xxii–xxiii.
25. Harris, *Lincoln's Last Months,* 107–110.
26. Ibid., 185–186.
27. Robert Selph Henry, *The Story of Reconstruction* (Indianapolis: Bobbs-Merrill, 1938), repr. (New York: Knockey & Knockey, 1999), 64.
28. Ibid.
29. Merton E. Coulter, *The South during Reconstruction: 1865–1877* (Baton Rouge: Louisiana State University Press, 1947), 7–10.
30. Harris, *Lincoln's Last Months,* 184–185.
31. Ibid., 185.
32. Selph, *Reconstruction,* 63.
33. Ibid., 63–64.
34. Ibid., 64–65.
35. Ibid., 64.

## Conclusion

1. Dattel, *Cotton and Race,* 61–85; "Government Revenue Details," USgovernmentrevnue.com, accessed August 3, 2013, www.usgovernmentrevenue.com/year_revenue_1860USmn_14ms1n_4046#usgs302.
2. Lebergott, "Why the South Lost," 72–73.
3. O'Connor, "Lincoln and the Cotton Trade," 32; Owsley, *King Cotton Diplomacy,* 289.
4. Stanley Lebergott, "Through the Blockade," *Journal of Economic History* 41, no. 4 (December 1981): 881.
5. House Commerce Committee, H. R. Summary Report No. 24, *Trade with the Rebellious States,* 38th Cong., 2nd sess., March 1, 1865.
6. "Consumer Price Index (Estimate) 1800–," Federal Reserve Bank of Minneapolis.
7. National Automobile Dealers Association, *NADA DATA: State-of-the-Industry Report 2013,* 3.

8. *Congressional Globe,* 38th Cong., 1st sess., vol. 2 (Washington, DC: 1864), 2823.
9. House Commerce Committee, *Trade with the Rebellious States,* 2.
10. Roberts, "Federal Government," 275.
11. Rhodes, *History of the Civil War,* 359.
12. McPherson, *Battle Cry,* 624–625.
13. Surdam, "Traders or Traitors," 303.
14. Gabor Boritt, *Lincoln and the Economics of the American Dream* (Urbana: University of Illinois Press, 1978), 243–247.
15. Harris, *Lincoln's Last Months,* 188.
16. McPherson, *Battle Cry,* 621.
17. Lamon, *Recollections of Abraham Lincoln,* 184–185. Cited in The Lincoln Institute, "Abraham Lincoln and Cotton," http://www.abrahamlincolnsclassroom.org/Library/newsletter.asp?ID=132&CRLI=180
18. Johnson, *Red River,* 50.
19. O'Connor, "Lincoln and the Cotton Trade," 26.
20. Ibid., 25.
21. Johnson, "Northern Profit," 114; Johnson, *Red River,* 71–74.
22. Rhodes, *History of the Civil War,* 359.

# BIBLIOGRAPHY


## Memoirs, Diaries, and Personal Papers

Bates, Edward. *Diary of Edward Bates.* Washington, DC: Government Printing Office, 1933.

Browning, Orville. *Diary of Orville Hickman Browning.* Springfield: Illinois State Historical Society, 1925.

Dana, Charles Anderson. *Recollections of the Civil War.* New York: D. Appleton, 1913.

Grant, Ulysses. *Personal Memoirs.* New York: Da Capo, 1952.

Howe, M. A. DeWolfe, ed. *Home Letters of General Sherman.* New York: Charles Scribner's Sons, 1909.

Johnson, B. T. "Memoir of the First Maryland Regiment." *Southern Historical Society Papers.* Vol. 9, 345–352.

Jones, John B. *A Rebel War Clerk's Diary.* 2 vols. Philadelphia: J. B. Lippincott, 1866.

Knox, Thomas W. *Campfire and Cotton Field.* New York: Bielock, 1865.

Lamon, Ward Hill. *Recollections of Abraham Lincoln.* Cambridge, MA: University Press, 1911.

Welles, Gideon. *Diary.* Vol. 1 Boston: Houghton, Mifflin, 1911.

## Historical Documents

*A Compilation of the Official Records of the Union and Confederate Navies in the War of Rebellion.* Washington, DC: Government Printing Office.

Congress of the Confederate States of America. *Statutes at Large.* Ch. 25, "An Act to Prohibit Dealing in the Paper Currency of the Enemy," February 6, 1864.

*Congressional Globe,* 38th Cong., 1st sess., vol. 2. Washington, DC: 1864.

Davis, Jefferson. Presidential inaugural address. February 18, 1861. Avalon Project, Lillian Goldman Law Library, Yale Law School. http://avalon.law.yale.edu/19th_century/csa_csainau.asp.

House Commerce Committee. H. R. Summary Report No. 24, *Trade with the Rebellious States*. 38th Cong., 2nd sess., March 1, 1865.

Lincoln, Abraham. Presidential inaugural address. March 4, 1861. Joint Congressional Committee on Inaugural Ceremonies. www.inaugural.senate.gov/swearing-in/address/address-by-abraham-lincoln-1865.

National Automobile Dealers Association, *NADA DATA: State-of-the-Industry Report 2013*.

*The War of the Rebellion: A Compilation of the Official Records of the Union and Confederate Armies*. Washington, DC: Government Printing Office.

## Books and Compilations

Adams, Charles. *When in the Course of Human Events*. Lanham, MD: Rowman & Littlefield, 2000.

Adams, Charles Francis, Jr. *Richard Henry Dana*. Boston: Houghton, Mifflin, 1891.

Anders, Curt. *Disaster in Damp Sand*. Carmel, IN: Guild Press, 1997.

Andreas, Peter. *Smuggler Nation*. Oxford: Oxford University Press, 2013.

Atkinson, Edward. *Cheap Cotton by Free Labor*. Boston: H. W. Dutton, 1861.

Ayers, Alex. *The Wit and Wisdom of Mark Twain*. New York: Meridian, 1989.

Bailey, Anne J., and Daniel E. Sutherland, eds. *Civil War Arkansas*. Fayetteville: University of Arkansas Press, 2000.

*The Blockade Runners and Raiders*. Chicago: Time-Life Books, 1983.

Boaz, Thomas. *Guns for Cotton*. Shippensburg, PA: Burd Street Press, 1996.

Bogue, Alan G. *The Congressman's Civil War*. Cambridge: Cambridge University Press, 1988.

Boritt, Gabor. *Lincoln and the Economics of the American Dream*. Urbana: University of Illinois Press, 1978.

Brooksher, William. *War along the Bayous*. Dulles, VA: Brassey's, 1998.

Cochran, Hamilton. *Blockade Runners*. Tuscaloosa: University of Alabama Press, 2005.

Cohn, David. *The Life and Times of King Cotton.* New York: Oxford University Press, 1956.

Coulter, Merton E. *The Confederate States of America: 1861–1865.* Baton Rouge: Louisiana State University Press, 1950.

———. *The South during Reconstruction: 1865–1877.* Baton Rouge: Louisiana State University Press, 1947.

Cowley, Charles. *Leaves from a Lawyer's Life Afloat and Ashore.* Lowell, MA: Penhallow, 1879.

Daddysman, James W. *The Matamoros Trade.* Newark: University of Delaware Press, 1984.

Dattel, Gene. *Cotton and Race in the Making of America.* Lanham, MD: Ivan R. Dee, 2009.

DeBlack, Thomas A. *With Fire and Sword.* Fayetteville: University of Arkansas Press, 2003.

Donald, David. *Lincoln.* London: Jonathan Cape, 1995.

Dougan, Michael B. *Confederate Arkansas.* Tuscaloosa: University of Alabama Press, 1991.

Durkin, Joseph T. *Confederate Navy Chief.* Columbia: University of South Carolina Press, 1954.

Eaton, Clement. *A History of the Southern Confederacy.* New York: Free Press, 1954.

Farrow, Anne, Joel Lang, and Jenifer Frank. *Complicity.* New York: Ballantine, 2005.

Flint, Henry Martyn. *Mexico under Maximilian.* Philadelphia: National Publishing, 1867.

Foner, Eric. *Reconstruction.* New York: Harper & Row, 1988.

Foreman, Amanda. *A World on Fire: Britain's Crucial Role in the American Civil War.* New York: Random House, 2010.

Hanna, Alfred, and Kathryn Hanna. *Napoleon III and Mexico.* Chapel Hill: University of North Carolina Press, 1971.

Harrington, Fred. *Fighting Politician.* Westport, CT: Greenwood, 1948.

Harris, William C. *Lincoln's Last Months.* Cambridge, MA: Harvard University Press, 2004.

Hart, Albert Bushnell. *Salmon Portland Chase.* Boston: Houghton, Mifflin, 1899.

Hearn, Chester G. *When the Devil Came Down to Dixie.* Baton Rouge: Louisiana State University Press, 1997.

Hendrick, Burton. *Statesmen of the Lost Cause.* New York: Literary Guild, 1939.

Henry, Robert Selph. *The Story of Reconstruction.* Indianapolis: Bobbs-Merrill, 1938. Reprint, New York: Knockey & Knockey, 1999.

Hollis, Christopher. *The American Heresy.* New York: Minton, Balch, 1930.

Horgan, James J. "A Confederate Bull in a Mexican China Shop." In John M. Belohlavek and Lewis N. Wynne, eds. *Divided We Fall: Essays on Confederate Nation Building.* St. Leo, FL: St. Leo College Press, 1991.

Johnson, Ludwell. *North against South: The American Iliad 1848–1877.* Columbia, SC: Foundation for American Education, 1995. Orig. publ. as *Division and Reunion: 1848–1877.* New York: John Wiley & Sons, 1978.

———. *Red River Campaign.* Kent, OH: Kent State University Press, 1993.

Joiner, Gary Dillard. *One Damn Blunder from Beginning to End.* Wilmington, DE: SR Books, 2003.

Jones, Robert A. *Confederate Corsair.* Mechanicsburg, PA: Stackpole Books, 2000.

Josephy, Alvin, Jr. *The Civil War in the American West.* New York: Alfred A. Knopf, 1991.

Kerby, Robert L. *Kirby Smith's Confederacy.* Tuscaloosa: University of Alabama Press, 1972.

Lamphier, Peg. *Kate Chase and William Sprague: Politics and Gender in a Civil War Marriage.* Lincoln: University of Nebraska Press, 2005.

Lieber, Francis. *Lieber's Code and the Law of War.* Chicago: Precedent, 1983.

Mahin, Dean B. *One War at a Time.* Washington, DC: Brassey's, 1999.

McPherson, James. *Battle Cry of Freedom.* London: Oxford University Press, 1988.

Miles, Donald. *Cinco de Mayo.* Lincoln, NE: iUniverse, 2006.

Miller, Nathan. *Theodore Roosevelt.* New York: William Morrow, 1992.

Moneyhon, Carl H. *The Impact of the Civil War and Reconstruction in Arkansas.* Baton Rouge: Louisiana State University Press, 1994.

Moore, Jerrold Northrop. *Confederate Commissary General.* Shippensburg, PA: White Mane, 1996.

Niven, John. *Salmon P. Chase.* Oxford: Oxford University Press, 1995.

Nulty, William H. *Confederate Florida: The Road to Olustee.* Tuscaloosa, University of Alabama Press, 1990.

Ochiai, Akiko. *Harvesting Freedom*. Westport, CT: Praeger, 2004.
O'Connor, Thomas H. *Lords of the Loom*. New York: Charles Scribner's Sons, 1968.
Owsley, Frank. *King Cotton Diplomacy*. Chicago: University of Chicago Press, 1931.
Pollard, Edward. *The Lost Cause*. Baltimore: E. B. Treat, 1883.
Powell, Lawrence N. *New Masters*. New York: Fordham University Press, 1998.
*The Record of Benjamin Butler from Original Sources*. Boston: pamphlet, 1883.
Rhodes, James Ford. *The History of the Civil War, 1861–1865*. New York: Macmillan, 1917.
———. *The History of the United States from the Compromise of 1850 to the Restoration of Home Rule*. Vol. 5. New York: Harper & Brothers, 1899.
Rose, Willie Lee. *Rehearsal for Reconstruction*. Athens: University of Georgia Press, 1999.
Simpson, Brooks. *Ulysses S. Grant*. Boston: Houghton Mifflin, 2000.
Smith, Andrew J. *Starving the South*. New York: St. Martin's Press, 2011.
Smith, Gene. *Maximilian and Carlotta*. London: Harrap, 1973.
Smith, Michael Thomas. *The Enemy Within*. Charlottesville: University Press of Virginia, 2011.
Stampp, Kenneth. *And the War Came*. Baton Rouge: Louisiana State University Press, 1970.
Surdam, David G. *Northern Naval Superiority and the Economics of the American Civil War*. Columbia: University of South Carolina Press, 2001.
Talese, Gay. *The Kingdom and the Power*. New York: Bantam, 1969.
Taylor, Richard. *Destruction and Reconstruction*. New York: Da Capo, 1995.
Thompson, Robert Means, and Richard Wainwright. *Confidential Correspondence of Gustavus Fox*. Vol. 1. New York: printed for the Naval History Society by De Vinne Press, 1918.
Wallace, Frederick A. *Civil War Hero: George H. Gordon*. Charleston, SC: History Press, 2011.
Walton, Gary M., and Hugh Rockoff. *History of the American Economy*. San Diego: Harcourt Brace Jovanovich, 1990.
Wiche, Glen N., ed. *Dispatches from Bermuda: The Civil War Letters of Charles Maxwell Allen, US Consul to Bermuda, 1861–1888*. Kent, OH: Kent State University Press, 2009.

Wiley, Bell Irvin. *Southern Negroes.* New York: Rinehart, 1938.
Wise, Stephen R. *Lifeline of the Confederacy.* Columbia: University of South Carolina Press, 1991.
Yafa, Stephen. *Cotton.* New York: Penguin, 2005.

Articles

Bailey, Ronald. "Slavery Trade and the Development of Capitalism in the USA: The Textile Industry in New England," *Social Science History* 14, no.3 (Autumn 1990): 373–414.
Bullard, Lauriston F. "Lincoln's Conquest of New England." *Abraham Lincoln Quarterly* 2, no. 2 (June 1942): 49–69.
Burdekin, Richard, and Farrokh K. Langdana. "War Finance in the Southern Confederacy: 1861–1865." *Explorations in Economic History* 30, no. 3 (1993): 352–376.
Coulter, Merton E. "Commercial Intercourse with the Confederacy in the Mississippi Valley 1861–1865." *Mississippi Valley Historical Review* 5, no. 4 (March 1919): 377–395.
Delaney, Robert W. "Matamoros: Port for Texas during the Civil War." *Southwestern Historical Quarterly* 58 (July 1954–April 1955): 473–487.
Gentry, Judith. "John A Stevenson: Confederate Adventurer." *Louisiana History* 35, no. 2 (1994): 151–161.
Johnson, Ludwell. "Blockade or Trade Monopoly?" *Virginia Magazine of History and Biography* 93, no. 1 (January 1985): 54–65.
———. "The Butler Expedition of 1861–1862: The Profitable Side of War." *Civil War History* 11, no. 3 (September 1965): 229–236.
———. "Commerce between Northeastern Ports and the Confederacy: 1861–1865." *Journal of American History* 54, no. 1 (June 1967): 30–42.
———. "Contraband Trade during the Last Year of the Civil War." *Mississippi Valley Historical Review* 91, no. 4 (March 1963): 635–652.
———. "Northern Profits and Profiteers: The Cotton Rings of 1864–1865." *Civil War History* 12, no. 2 (June 1966): 101–115.
———. "Trading with the Union: The Evolution of Confederate Policy." *Virginia Magazine of History and Biography* 78, no. 3 (July 1970): 308–325.
Jones, Francis I. W. "This Fraudulent Trade." (*Canadian) Northern Mariner* 9, no. 4 (October 1999): 35–46.
Lebergott, Stanley. "Through the Blockade." *Journal of Economic History* 41, no. 4 (December 1981): 867–888.

———. "Why the South Lost: Commercial Purpose in the Confederacy: 1861–1865." *Journal of American History* 70, no. 1 (June 1983): 58–74.

Marquis, Greg. "The Ports of Halifax and St. Johns and the American Civil War." *(Canadian) Northern Mariner* 7, no.1 (January 1998): 1–19.

Oates, Stephen. "John S. 'Rip' Ford." *Southwestern Historical Quarterly* 64, no. 3 (January 1961): 289–314.

Ochiai, Akiko. "The Port Royal Experiment Revisited." *New England Quarterly* 74, no. 1 (March 2001): 94–117.

O'Connor, Thomas. "Lincoln and the Cotton Trade." *Civil War History* 7, no. 1 (March 1961): 20–35.

Peters, Thelma. "Blockade-Running in the Bahamas during the Civil War." Paper read before the Historical Association of Southern Florida, May 5, 1943.

Roberts, A. Sellew. "The Federal Government and Confederate Cotton." *American Historical Review* 32, no. 2 (January 1927): 262–275.

Sibley, Marilyn. "Charles Stillman: A Case Study of Entrepreneurship on the Rio Grande, 1861–1865." *Southwestern Historical Quarterly* 77, no. 2 (October 1973): 227–240.

Smith, George Winston. "Cotton from Savannah in 1865." *Journal of Southern History* 21, no. 4 (November 1955): 495–512.

Surdam, David G. "Traders or Traitors: Northern Cotton Trading During the Civil War." *Business and Economic History* 28, no. 2 (Winter 1999): 301–312.

Tyler, Ronnie C. "Cotton on the Border, 1861–1865." *Southwestern Historical Quarterly* 73, no. 4 (April 1970): 456–477.

## Dissertations

Futrell, Robert F. "Federal Trade with the Confederate States: 1861–1865." PhD diss.,Vanderbilt University, 1950.

## Web sites

American Historical Association. "Editorials of Secession Project." *Chicago Daily Times*, December 10, 1860. http://historians.org/projects/secessioneditorials/Editorials/ChicagoTimes_12_10_60.htm.

Badger, Emily. "Of Course the Civil War Was about Slavery," *Pacific Standard*, December 20, 2010. www.psmag.com/culture-society/of-course-the-civil-war-was-about-slavery-26265/.

Blight, David, "Slavery and State Rights, Economies and Ways of Life: What Caused the Civil War?" Lecture no. 11, Yale University, History-119 ("The Civil War and Reconstruction Era, 1845–1877"), February 19, 2008. http://oyc.yale.edu/transcript/552/hist-119.

Burton, Orville, and Patricia Bonnin. "The Confederacy," *Macmillan Information Now Encyclopedia.* www.civilwarhome.com/kingcotton.htm.

Federal Reserve Bank of Minneapolis, "Consumer Price Index (Estimate) 1800–." www.minneapolisfed.org/community_education/teacher/calc/hist1800.cfm?.

"Forget Lincoln Logs: A Tower of Books to Honor Abe." Interview with Paul Tetreault. National Public Radio, February 20, 2012. www.npr.org/2012/02/20/147062501/forget-lincoln-logs-a-tower-of-books-to-honor-abe.

Gilder Lehrman Institute of American History. *Confederate Act to Authorize the Exporting of Produce and Merchandise.* www.gilderlehrman.org/collections/590534e9-fb05-44c7-a976-099992402122?back=/mweb/search%3Fpage%3D4%2526needle%3DTobacco%2520and%2520Smoking%253B%2526fields%3D_t301001410.

"Government Revenue Details." www.usgovernmentrevenue.com/numbers.

Hart, John Mason. "Stillman, Charles." *Handbook of Texas Online.* Texas State Historical Association. www.tshaonline.org/handbook/online/articles/fst57.

———. "Stillman, James." *Handbook of Texas Online.* Texas State Historical Association. www.tshaonline.org/handbook/online/articles/fstbp.

*Historical Statistics of the United States: Colonial Times to 1970,* Part 1. US Department of Commerce, Bureau of the Census. www2.census.gov/prod2/statcomp/documents/CT1970p1-01.pdf.

Leigh, Phil. "Trading with the Enemy," *New York Times* Opinionator, October 28, 2012. http://opinionator.blogs.nytimes.com/2012/10/28/trading-with-the-enemy/.

Lincoln Institute. "Abraham Lincoln and Cotton." www.abrahamlincolnsclassroom.org/Library/newsletter.asp?ID=132&CRLI=180.

Lockwood, John, and Charles Lockwood. "First South Carolina. Then New York?" *New York Times* Opinionator, January 6, 2011. http://opinionator.blogs.nytimes.com/2011/01/06/first-south-carolina-then-new-york/.

McPherson, James. "Second Thoughts on the Civil War as a Second Revolution." *Hayes Historical Journal* 3, no. 5 (Spring 1982). www.rbhayes.org/hayes/content/files/Hayes_Historical_Journal/somethoughts.htm.

Shapiro, Michael. "Rehearsal for Reconstruction." *New York Times* Opinionator, September 6, 2011. http://opinionator.blogs.nytimes.com/2011/11/06/rehearsal-for-reconstruction/.

Stone, Benjamin. "Excerpts Selected from James McPherson's Works: Finding a Dissertation Topic." Stanford University Libraries and Academic Information Sources, 2009. http://prelectur.stanford.edu/lecturers/mcpherson/excerpts.html.

Wilson, William Moss. "The Confederate of the Sierra Madre." *New York Times* Opinionator, September 1, 2011. http://opinionator.blogs.nytimes.com/2011/09/01/the-confederate-of-the-sierra-madre/.

# INDEX